# THE TEACHER'S GUIDE
# TO SELF-CARE

*The*

# TEACHER'S GUIDE TO SELF-CARE

## Build Resilience, Avoid Burnout, and Bring a Happier and Healthier You to the Classroom

### SARAH FORST

First edition: July 2020

Cover Design: Jasmine Hromjak
Interior Design: Jennifer Toomey
Editor: Stephanie Carbajal
Author Photo: Erin Drewitz

ISBN 978-1-7353337-0-0 (paperback)
ISBN 978-1-7353337-1-7 (ebook)

Published by The Designer Teacher, LLC
thedesignerteacher.com

# CONTENTS

# INTRODUCTION

Teaching is one of the most important and fulfilling jobs in the world. And yet, teacher burnout is all too common—and many teachers find themselves sacrificing their own mental health for the sake of their jobs. Do you feel exhausted, over-whelmed, and stressed-out much of the time? You're not alone. But teaching doesn't *have* to be this way. Practicing self-care is critical to building resilience and creating a sustainable career as a teacher.

In this book, you'll learn what self-care is and why it's so important for teachers. You'll also discover practical strategies for making time for self-care, setting boundaries, and becoming a healthier and happier teacher. Whether you're a brand-new teacher preparing for your first year in the classroom or a veteran educator realizing you need to take better care of yourself, *The Teacher's Guide to Self-Care* will help you create the self-care routines you need for a sustainable career. Leave the teacher-martyr complex behind and embrace a lifestyle that includes taking care of yourself physically, mentally, and spiritually while continuing to make a difference in the world.

As a former special education teacher in Chicago Public Schools and the creator of the self-care subscription box for teachers, Teacher Care Crate, I know the importance of teacher self-care firsthand. After experiencing a mental breakdown as a young teacher, I became passionate about helping other teachers avoid the same pitfalls and become the best teachers they can be *without* sacrificing their well-being. While not currently in the classroom, I strive to help teachers every day through meaningful classroom resources in my Teachers Pay Teachers store, The Designer Teacher, reminders to practice self-care through Teacher Care Crate, and now, this book.

I'm so glad you've opened *The Teacher's Guide to Self-Care*, and I can't wait to go on this journey with you. Let's get started!

# HOW TO USE THIS BOOK

I wrote this book to be accessible and actionable. You can start here and read it straight through, or, if you prefer, you can page through to the sections that are most applicable to you. I do recommend that you take the self-care quiz on p. 26 to get an idea of how you're currently doing with your self-care before you begin.

If you do read this guide straight through, keep in mind that you can always come back to certain sections when you need to. You might want to reread the affirmations (p. 64) after a rough day, or flip to the journaling section (p. 68) when you're in the mood to write.

If you're reading a physical copy of this book, you may want to read with a pen or highlighter so you can mark the ideas you want to implement. If you're reading a digital copy or don't want to mark up your book, keep a notebook nearby so you can make a running list of the ideas that appeal to you. You may also wish to use a notebook to answer the reflection questions at the end of most sections.

## MY STORY

As a college student getting a fine arts degree in interdisciplinary object design, I didn't exactly plan on becoming a teacher. Yet

I wanted to help people in a concrete way, and designing drills or working for a 3-D modeling company weren't particularly appealing options to me as an idealistic twenty-two-year-old. I've always enjoyed working with kids, so I decided to apply for the alternative certification program Teach for America (TFA) and see what happened. I was thrilled to be accepted and even more thrilled to learn I was placed in Chicago, where my then-boyfriend, now-husband, lived. After graduating, I took part in TFA's six-week summer "institute" (commonly called TFA boot camp by members), which consisted of packed days of professional development, mentoring, teaching summer school, and beginning grad school. I was hired by a charter school on the far south side of Chicago as a special education teacher and would begin teaching with only a provisional certification.

I began the school year with high hopes, knowing it would be hard work, but truly wanting to make a difference in the world. It wasn't quite like *The Wire* or what some other "inner-city school" narratives make it out to be. The school itself wasn't a scary place to me (though the four-block walk from the train through a gang boundary was a little nerve-wracking), and most teachers seemed well-intentioned.

I received a schedule of when I should pull kids for special education services, and when I should "push in" for inclusion services. I found myself thinking, "And now what?" I truly had no idea what I was supposed to be doing with students when I brought them to the resource room. While I may have been underprepared due to the alternative teaching certification I received through TFA, I've heard from many traditional special education teachers that they were also not taught what to teach. So I started with the basics and began to teach them to read. The school had a few resources here and there—old textbooks and a handful of PDFs of worksheets—but nothing like what I actually needed for teaching students with disabilities how to read. I searched online, I ordered phonics books, but ultimately I mostly created my own materials to teach my students how to read.

As a charter school employee, I was required to arrive twenty minutes before school began and stay for thirty minutes after. I usually arrived long before and left long after. Three days a week, I took the train directly downtown for three hours of graduate school to get my full special education certification. On those days, I arrived home around 10 p.m. and collapsed, exhausted, only to repeat the routine the next day. But I was young and motivated and I survived. I loved my students and it was truly incredible to watch them learn how to read after years of stagnation.

By first-year teacher standards, I suppose I was doing well. I was nominated for a nationwide teacher award within Teach for America. My principal liked me. Still, I considered not going back the next year. I hadn't known much about charter schools before then, and I saw the damage they were doing within the Chicago education landscape after working at one for a year— and knowing many others who also did. Still, I wanted to finish my Teach for America commitment to staying at my school, so I returned for an additional year, despite having a longer school year and longer school days and making $10,000 less a year than my Chicago Public Schools counterparts.

After my two-year commitment, I entered the Chicago Public Schools system and began teaching at an elementary school in the Rogers Park neighborhood of Chicago. The teachers there were more experienced, and the strong Chicago Teachers Union meant we weren't required to work outside of contract hours and were entitled to our sick days and prep periods. I felt more confident and less tired, with a much shorter commute and no grad school to worry about. I enjoyed my work and I think I was a good teacher.

Things should have gotten better. And yet, I was always on the brink of a mental breakdown. In October of my second year at the school in Rogers Park, I had the breakdown that had been looming since I began teaching. I felt that no matter what I did, it wouldn't be good enough. I had created my own phonics curriculum the year before. I had spent weeks setting up my classroom. I even already knew most of my students that year. Still, like most teachers, I was being asked to do more than I could possibly do during school hours. And I've never been one to do the bare minimum, so I often continued working from the moment school ended until it was time to go to sleep. Each task felt urgent—and sometimes it was. IEPs *do* need to be finished, lesson plans turned in, centers made. But I had trouble feeling like it was ever, ever enough.

That fall, I received my first less-than-stellar observation scores from the new assistant principal, and I was devastated. It turned out to be a fluke because she gave universally bad scores for all first observations that year and, in fact, the principal tried to make up for it by giving me wildly inflated scores for my next observation. Still, that initial observation confirmed what I already thought privately: I wasn't doing a good enough job. Part of me felt ashamed for not being good enough, as good as my students deserved. However, I was also enraged that I didn't have the tools needed to be successful, from copy paper to time to write IEPs.

Embarrassingly, I found myself crying to someone just about every day. If the topic of work was brought up, I started crying. I cried as I tried to finish one last thing before going to sleep, even though I was exhausted and hadn't taken a break all day. I cried when my mom asked how I was doing. I felt so overwhelmed all the time that the littlest thing could set me off.

Various people in my life told me, "You're doing your best," and "You've done enough." But my response, whether verbally or in my own head was, "But I'm *not* doing my best. It's *never* enough." I thought if only I could stay up later or get to school earlier or write my lesson plans further ahead of time, maybe *that* would be enough.

One day, I was sick but went to school anyway because I felt it was impossible for me to miss a day. I was so distraught and feverish that I ate in my room at lunch instead of the teachers' lounge. I was huddled under my desk, quietly sobbing, when my speech pathologist friend came looking for me. She told me I was going home, signed me out with my ID so I wouldn't have to face the front office with red eyes, and emailed my principal and co-teachers to let them know I'd gone home sick. I still feel a bit ashamed recounting this years later, but I'm thankful for this incident, because it gave me the necessary wake-up call to know I needed help.

I've known I have Generalized Anxiety Disorder since high school, and I began taking SSRIs, a common anxiety and depression medication, in college. I never sought out regular therapy because I always felt (and appeared to be) high-functioning and didn't think I needed it. When I found myself teetering on the edge of my mental breakdown, it was clear that the time had come.

I don't quite remember what specifically prompted me to find a therapist, but I'm so thankful that I did. I will be forever grateful to my therapist for her much-needed perspective, and I hope I can provide a fraction of the insight to you that she provided to me. In one of my first sessions, she asked what I did for self-care. Slightly confused by the question (self-care wasn't as much of a buzzword then as it is now!), I said that I slept and I ran. "Those don't count," she said.

My therapy homework was to spend ten minutes twice a week doing nothing. "Nothing" could mean meditating, coloring, or any activity in which I wasn't working or trying to reach a goal. I genuinely felt I did not have time for twenty minutes a week of nothing. There are 10,080 minutes a week, and I felt I didn't have twenty. But I did the homework, because I'm nothing if not someone who knows how to follow instructions. Twice a week, when I got home from school, before I picked up my laptop to begin working again, I sat down at the dining room table and did some coloring in an adult coloring book. Later, I began to do jigsaw puzzles, which is still one of my favorite forms of self-care. As I did the work, I began to notice that I was more relaxed and able to focus better later when I took those ten-minute breaks. On the days I took them, I looked forward to the breaks and felt like I could work on tasks more efficiently afterward. I began to crave these breaks and started to take them most days, slowly increasing the total time to thirty minutes. It felt rebellious, taking time for myself with no purpose.

My therapist told me I was quite literally working myself to death at twenty-six years old. It may sound harsh, but I needed someone to tell me that. I took it seriously and I'm so glad I did. I began to be less angry at myself, and more at the system and what was asked of me. The overwhelm and intense anxiety began to shift into burnout. I wasn't crying every day anymore; instead I felt bitter and frustrated. I wanted to finish the school year, as I knew it would be extremely difficult for my school to find a new special education teacher midyear, but I decided I would not return the following year.

I resigned when the school year ended and decided to take a few months off before starting a new job. I spent that time working on my Teachers Pay Teachers (TPT) store, a venture I had started several years before. As my TPT income grew, I realized I was close to matching my teacher salary and continued to work from home and grow my business. Later that year, I began Teacher Care Crate, my self-care subscription for teachers. Out of my own experience in the world of education

I found my passion: helping other teachers take care of themselves so they can, in turn, take better care of their students.

While I hope your experience hasn't been as extreme as mine, I have no doubt that you identify with parts of it. Having been out of the classroom for several years, I see more clearly than ever how unreasonable the demands placed on teachers are, and how dire the need is for self-care.

Now that you know my story, let's begin our journey into self-care.

## Part 1

# WHAT IS SELF-CARE?

Self-care is, quite simply, taking care of yourself. It should be the most obvious and important thing we do as human beings. But for many teachers, we spend our days taking care of others instead of ourselves, from beginning to end.

Consider a common day in the life of a teacher: Wake at 6 a.m., after likely getting less than the recommended eight hours of sleep. Quickly get ready for your day, skipping breakfast or grabbing a snack on your way out. Take your coffee to go—possibly more than you should, just to stay awake on your drive to work. Arrive at school before contract hours start to make copies and prep for the day's activities. Teach through the morning, eat a frozen meal heated in the microwave for lunch. (The health inspector called the condition of the microwave at my last school "deplorable.") Make some more copies, try to squeeze in time to go to the bathroom, and pick up your students. If you get allotted prep time, you may spend it lesson planning or grading, or you may be required to sacrifice your only planning time for a team meeting or IEP meeting. You finish your day with your students, likely talking to parents after school. You may run a club or sport, or you may just stay for an hour or two or more trying to get ready for the next day. You head home, have dinner, and take care of any errands or household tasks. You respond to coworker, school, and parent emails. You finish any last-minute planning for the next day. You collapse into bed around midnight. You wake up six hours later and repeat.

This may sound pretty grim, and it certainly doesn't highlight the many rewarding aspects of teaching, but it is the reality for many teachers, especially those in under-resourced schools. This example also doesn't consider that many teachers are parents, with their own children to care for as well!

Let's look at some of the points throughout the day when a stressed-out teacher could take better care of him- or herself.

**Sleep:** Adults need a minimum of seven hours of sleep to function correctly, and many need more. As a teacher, I was really diligent about getting eight hours of sleep, but I was still exhausted every day. After I stopped teaching, I discovered I need nine hours to be at my best. When a teacher gets less sleep than they need, it impacts their happiness and likely their job performance as well.

**Food:** We all know that well-rounded meals with plenty of fruits and vegetables are healthiest, and your average teacher may not have the time, money, or energy to eat these kinds of meals regularly.

**Exercise:** On an average school day, it's hard to squeeze in a workout. And if you do, it can feel like it's at the expense of something else.

**Personal Time:** This may be the most likely aspect of self-care your average teacher is missing. For many, it feels the least essential, so we don't take time for ourselves.

If a teacher repeats this schedule every day for weeks on end, he or she is on the path to burnout.

Self-care encompasses all areas of taking care of yourself, including physical, emotional, social, intellectual, vocational, and environmental. We will go into each area in more detail later, but as teachers, many of us first need to shift our mindset from seeing self-care as selfish to seeing it as necessary.

## SELF-CARE ISN'T SELFISH

I was delighted to come across the term "altruistic egotism" while doing research for this book. This term was coined way back in 1974 in the book *Stress Without Distress*[1] by Hans Selye. It suggests that taking care of ourselves can actually be altruistic. In their book *The Resilient Practitioner: Burnout and Compassion Fatigue Prevention and Self-Care Strategies for the Helping Professions*, Skovholt and Trotter-Mathison state, "The individual must hold his or her own welfare as a holy or sacred obligation."[2] I love this. A sacred obligation. Do you see taking care of yourself as a sacred obligation? I know I didn't. I felt like my talents, my hard work, even my physical body should be completely used up for others. Making the shift from seeing self-care as selfish to seeing it as a sacred obligation is powerful.

One of the most meaningful experiences of my life was living and volunteering in a home for sick children in Peru as a nineteen-year-old for three months. After living in the privileged bubble of a white suburban community, and then experiencing two years of college that was still relatively white and privileged, doing real, concrete work was incredibly meaningful. I was quite literally getting my hands dirty, washing forty sets of dirty dishes by hand, emptying *papagayos* (urine containers for boys who could not easily reach the bathroom), and navigating completely inaccessible Lima with kids with significant disabilities.

---

1   Hans Selye, *Stress without Distress* (United Kingdom: McClelland and Stewart, 1974).

2   Thomas M. Skovholt and Michelle Trotter-Mathison, *The Resilient Practitioner: Burnout and Compassion Fatigue Prevention and Self-Care Strategies for the Helping Professions*, 3rd ed. (New York: Routledge, 2016), 128.

The man in charge, Dr. Tony, was an American doctor who turned his life around to run this home, day in and day out, year after year. He was already old when I was there ten years ago. The kids told me he used to play soccer with them, but when I was there, he was more than a little cranky and spent most of the day in his office. Still, his incredible dedication to the forty-plus kids in his care at any given time was astonishing. He is the closest I have ever met to a hero. Today, a more cynical and social justice–versed me could cast a critical light on the whole operation, from white saviorism to voluntourism. But honestly, it was and is the real deal. I wanted to be like Dr. Tony. My time spent in Peru set me on my path to becoming a special education teacher. But I've learned that the Dr. Tonys of the world are few and far between.

What was supposed to be a four-month trip was reduced to three after I got severe pneumonia. I was so sick I couldn't fly, despite my parents begging me to come home, so I convalesced for about two weeks or so before going home. Another volunteer died while I was there, and for the next year I had dreams of falling, falling, falling, just like my friend fell off a roof and died. It took my body a long time to recover from pneumonia and get back up to a healthy weight. My digestive system and teeth were wrecked from food poisoning and lack of fluoride. I couldn't eat dairy for months, and I had—wait for it—NINE cavities. You would've thought I'd develop an understanding of the need for self-care from that trip, but I didn't. I repeated these mistakes as a teacher, albeit on a different scale and in a different setting.

After years of dedicating my every waking hour of teaching, I bumped up against a wall. It wasn't a matter of *wanting* to continue, it was a matter of *not being able* to continue. Maybe the Dr. Tonys of the world are just superior human beings.

Maybe I don't know the whole story. Either way, I'm relieved that the research on self-care and burnout backs me up. My mindset of being a martyr, and then suffering burnout as a consequence, is all too common among teachers. As I read a case study on a burnt-out teacher in Maslach and Leiter's *The Truth About Burnout*, I got chills. Julie was a young, successful, highly praised teacher, and then, surprising all her coworkers, she quits. "To Julie, trying to do good came at too high a price."[3] This is exactly how I felt at the end of my last year of teaching. All my life, I wanted to help people. I didn't know I was capable of reaching a point at which the price was too high, but I was. I'm not a martyr, and I discovered through therapy that I don't want to be. I want to have a pleasant and meaningful homelife. I want to have pets or kids, to have a home I love, to travel, to have time for hobbies. These desires don't make you a bad person. They make you, quite simply, a person.

You're not a saint. You're not a martyr. And you don't have to be. In fact, "altruistic egotism," or in other words, self-care, is what can allow you to have a long, healthy career in which you can take care of yourself AND others. A recent study found that only 7 percent of teachers reported both low levels of stress and high levels of coping with their jobs.[4] With numbers like these, it's hardly surprising that nearly half of new teachers leave the profession within five years.[5] While it's important to advocate for structural changes that will decrease teacher

---

3    Christina Maslach and Michael P. Leiter, *The Truth About Burnout: How Organizations Cause Personal Stress and What to Do About It* (San Francisco: Jossey-Bass, 1997), 25.

4    Keith C. Herman, Jal'et Hickmon-Rosa, and Wendy M. Reinke, "Empirically Derived Profiles of Teacher Stress, Burnout, Self-Efficacy, and Coping and Associated Student Outcomes," *Journal of Positive Behavior Interventions* 20, no. 2 (April 1, 2018): 90, https://doi.org/10.1177/1098300717732066.

5    Richard M. Ingersoll, Elizabeth Merrill, Daniel Stuckey, and Gregory Collins, "Seven Trends: The Transformation of the Teaching Force," *CPRE Research Reports* November 13, 2018, https://repository.upenn.edu/cpre_researchreports/108.

stress levels in schools, it's also clear that teachers who want to stay in the profession long-term need to practice self-care in order to decrease their stress and ability to cope.

> *"A good teacher is like a candle—it consumes itself to light the way for others."*
>
> —MUSTAFA KEMAL ATATÜRK

If you can believe it, this quote was included in a popular teacher planner as recently as the 2018–19 school year. The idea that teachers need to sacrifice themselves for their students is considered so commonplace, and even innocuous, that it can be hand-lettered and placed in a teacher planner as if it's inspiring. Mindsets like this run rampant throughout the school system. From movies like *Stand by Me* to *Freedom Writers*, the teacher-martyr is celebrated. Many begin teaching because we do, in fact, want to help people. Perhaps partially because teaching is a female-dominated profession, being a teacher is sometimes treated as a volunteer position. Teachers are asked regularly to stay past working/contract hours and are expected to do so without complaint—because after all, we're in it for the outcome, not the income, right?

I do believe most teachers teach out of a desire to help others, because teaching wouldn't be your chosen profession if your goal was to make a ton of money. But when we act as if teachers shouldn't care about their salaries or themselves at all, we're doing the whole school system a disservice. I stand with teachers and I believe that you, regardless of your job or test scores, deserve to be healthy and happy. But even if our principals, superintendents, and politicians don't care about teachers' well-being for their well-being's sake alone, they SHOULD care because it affects our students and our schools. Teacher burnout is rampant across the United States, and the statistics are even more dire in schools with historically underserved students. In fact, teacher turnover rates are 50 percent higher for teachers in Title I schools and 70 percent higher in the schools with the highest concentrations of students of color.[6] Personal teacher self-care will not solve the structural problems of education or society's unfair expectations for teachers. However, it will hopefully at least allow you personally to have a happier, healthier, and more sustainable career in education.

## UNDERSTANDING SELF-CARE
### Not Everything That Feels Good Is Self-Care: Self-Care vs. Self-Soothing

Before we get into the details of specific forms of self-care, I feel the need to specify what *isn't* self-care. In doing research for this book, I came across several images and articles that defined self-care as anything that feels good. I vehemently disagree with that idea. When we think of self-care as a sacred obligation, we realize that doing whatever feels good *in the moment* isn't necessarily self-care. Self-care *can* and often does feel good, but when something feels good, but isn't good *for* you, that's self-soothing, not self-care.

Self-soothing is not inherently bad. Just as you might try to soothe an upset student, it's okay to soothe yourself. However, we need to be aware that self-soothing isn't a replacement for self-care, and extensive self-soothing can be a form of avoidance. For example, you might soothe a crying student by letting them curl up with a pillow in the library area for a little bit. However, you wouldn't let them do that all day. Ultimately, you care for the student by asking them to return to learning with the rest of the class. We must treat ourselves the same way. We can soothe ourselves to a reasonable extent, but then

---

6    Desiree Carver-Thomas and Linda Darling-Hammond, "Teacher Turnover: Why It Matters and What We Can Do About It," Learning Policy Institute, August 16, 2017, https://learningpolicyinstitute.org/product/teacher-turnover-report.

we need to return to actually caring for ourselves and doing what's good for us. When it comes to teachers, I've noticed three main forms of self-soothing being touted as self-care that aren't actually good for you: alcohol, sugar, and television.

» *ALCOHOL*

Wine is a pretty big part of teacher culture. There's nothing wrong with having a glass of wine for most people—I do so myself many nights—and hey, there are even health benefits to drinking red wine! Enjoying a drink or two to relax or because you like the taste isn't a problem for most people. But binge drinking, which the Centers for Disease Control and Prevention defines as four or more drinks for women and five or more for men, isn't healthy, and it isn't self-care. When you feel like you *have* to get drunk on the weekend to blow off steam, that's an indicator that you're not coping. If you frequently drink so much that you get sick or don't remember the events of the night before, alcohol has become the opposite of self-care.

» *SUGAR*

The same goes for sugary coffee drinks and other treats. There was a drive-thru Starbucks on the way home from school my second year of teaching, and the urge would be so strong to stop and get a cinnamon dolce latte. It would've felt good to give in and get one every single day. But that wouldn't have been good for my bank account or my health. A grande cinnamon dolce latte contains 41 grams of sugar—nearly twice the recommended sugar intake for women for the whole day! Why was the craving so powerful? Because I wasn't caring for myself in any other way. I was sleep- and nutrient- deprived and I just wanted anything that would make me feel good.

Examine these urges in yourself, whether it's alcohol, sugar, or something else, and find an alternative for those that aren't truly good for you. Today, I have minimal sugar in my everyday life, but I do have treats on holidays and vacations—I'm not skipping Belgian waffles in Belgium or pumpkin pie on Thanksgiving! If what you're treating yourself with is actually bad for you, try to come up with a replacement, or make some other adjustments in your life that will reduce the craving.

» *TELEVISION*

Binging on TV is another oft-touted form of self-care that actually isn't. I think we can cross pretty much anything with "binge" in front of it off the self-care list. It feels good to lie on the couch all day and watch Netflix, but how do you feel after? Do you feel refreshed and reenergized? I certainly don't. I know I would feel better if I spent the day hiking or, for a day that's more restful, sleeping in, reading a book at a coffee shop, or practicing a healthy hobby.

Of course, this is just my personal experience with binge watching television, so I was curious to see what the research had to say. One study found that people do experience a sense of relaxation while watching television, but the sense of relaxation ends very quickly after they stop watching. This is not the case with other activities, such as reading, playing sports, or practicing a hobby. After watching TV, the participants in the study had less energy and felt less alert. Interestingly, the same study found that people who watched more TV enjoyed it less than "light viewers" (two hours or less a day).[7] So it seems that if your goal is to relax or improve your mood in a lasting way, you are better off practicing a different form of relaxation. When you do watch TV, you'll likely experience maximum enjoyment if you watch for two hours or less at a time.

---

7    Robert Kubey, and Mihaly Csikszentmihalyi, "Television Addiction Is No Mere Metaphor," *Scientific American* 286, no. 2 (March 2002): 51.

While alcohol, sugar, and television are the forms of self-soothing I see most often among teachers, there are certainly others. If you are avoiding a coworker you're having issues with, that's self-soothing rather than self-care. It feels good not to face your coworker, and you might need to do that while you're still actively upset. But once you've calmed down, the best way to practice emotional self-care is likely to talk it out with your coworker and express yourself, even though that might be scary and not feel good in the moment.

As someone with anxiety, I often self-soothe by staying home. Staying home is pretty much always going to be what feels best for me in the moment. I don't like driving, I can't stand the social awkwardness of using a rideshare service, and I experience motion sickness on public transit. What feels good to me is staying home with my dogs. But I know I need to practice social self-care by getting out, seeing my friends, and interacting with the world. When I started working from home, my therapist pointed out that I was developing avoidant behaviors, like always having my husband go to the store. So I know that it's also taking care of my mental health to get out into the world, even when it would feel better in the moment to stay home. For an extroverted person, this is likely not an issue. Instead, they might self-soothe by always being around people and not taking time for personal reflection and to get in touch with themselves.

Take a few minutes to reflect on your own habits and personality and determine whether those habits are forms of self-soothing or self-care. Remember, you don't need to eliminate self-soothing habits completely, but just make sure you're practicing them in moderation.

## What Makes Self-Care So Challenging for Teachers to Practice?

*"The best thing about being a teacher is that it matters. The hardest thing about being a teacher is that it matters every day."*

—TODD WHITAKER

This quote pretty much sums up why it's so challenging for teachers to practice self-care. We don't have the luxury of sitting at a desk and not seeing or knowing who our work directly affects. We are painfully aware of the challenges our schools and students face. For teachers, especially those who have anxiety, every task can feel urgent. We see the direct consequences of our actions or lack of actions every day in the students sitting in our classroom. And we're not wrong. Education is urgent, especially if you're teaching students who are at a disadvantage in the world.

On top of the world's most important task—educating the future—we are asked to do what feels like a million other tasks: be on committees, change out bulletin boards monthly, make copies, input grades, call parents, run clubs, write IEPs, attend professional development. Just writing out that list makes me want to shout, "There's not enough time! There's never enough time!" And I believe that to be true. There genuinely is not enough time for the modern teacher to do all the things she is tasked with. And so, we must be ruthless in what we cut from our schedules, we must prioritize wisely, and we must be protective of our mental health.

When someone in your life suggests you need to take better care of yourself, a million reasons why you can't probably come to mind. Here are a few of the most common excuses we come up with for not practicing self-care—and the rebuttals.

*Excuse: "I don't have time."*

**Rebuttal:** If you truly feel like every minute of your day is booked, something must be cut. Maybe that means grading fewer assignments, dropping a committee, or purchasing a unit plan instead of creating one. You have to choose something, because you can't continue running on empty forever.

*Excuse: "{insert task here} is more important."*

**Rebuttal:** The task may be important, but ultimately, taking care of yourself is the task that allows you to complete all other tasks. You're not going to function well or complete tasks correctly if you're not taking care of yourself.

*Excuse: "I should be able to handle this."*

**Rebuttal:** Teaching is an extraordinarily difficult job, even in the best of circumstances. You are a human being, not a superhero. There is nothing wrong with needing rest.

*Excuse: "I'm putting my students first."*

**Rebuttal:** What's good for teachers is good for students. Taking care of yourself is a way of taking care of your students. Practicing self-care allows you to be at your best.

Most American schools are, ahem, not exactly set up as a healthy environment for their teachers. I've seen some push-back on self-care from the education community. To paraphrase, essentially the critique is: *bubble baths won't make teachers more valued or better paid.* Ain't that the truth. And yet, as Skovolt and Trotter-Mathison warn in *The Resilient Practitioner,*

"Be careful about waiting for others to care for you."[8] I absolutely believe in advocating for the rights of teachers. Work in a state with a strong union, or help build one. Personal self-care is not a solution for the enormous burdens placed on teachers nationwide. And yet, you have your own well-being to consider. Advocate for yourself and all teachers, but don't let that stop you from taking care of yourself first. We can work on changing the system while still taking care of ourselves. A bubble bath won't improve your working conditions, but it may help you face school with a calmer and more peaceful mindset.

### Why Is Self-Care So Important for Teachers?

Self-care is important for all human beings, but I believe it to be even more important for teachers. Our state of mind and well-being has a direct effect on our students, and thus, the future of our world. We might feel that by working ourselves to the brink of exhaustion or a mental breakdown we're helping our students, but in fact, we're not.

Kids are intuitive, and they often know when their teacher doesn't want to be at school. They might even know when you're just stressed or upset. As a special education teacher, I did a feelings check-in with my students at the beginning of every class. They frequently anticipated that I was feeling stressed or anxious before I said so. You might be able to put on a cheerful facade for students, but that's draining in and of itself, and it won't last forever.

Teacher stress and burnout affects students daily, but it affects them most when the teaching profession loses another talented teacher. You cannot last by giving 150 percent—I know from experience. I doubt you could find a supervisor, coworker, or student of mine who didn't think I was extremely dedicated. But everyone has that breaking point when they just can't take

---

8    Skovholt and Trotter-Mathison, *The Resilient Practitioner,* 107.

it anymore, even with the best of intentions. I hope this book can help you avoid reaching that breaking point, or, if you're already there, I hope it can help you take a step back and begin to reshape your life.

If you're a new teacher, the chance that you won't make it as a teacher long-term is especially high. More than 44 percent of all new teachers leave teaching within the first five years.[9] So, if you're feeling overwhelmed, or like this job is just too hard, you don't have to feel guilty or that you're not good enough. That is the job. It's not just you. While systemic changes are needed, this book focuses on what *you* can do to create a sustainable career.

Self-care can decrease your stress, thus helping you have a longer career as a teacher and avoid burnout. One study even found that engaged and resilient teachers have better instructional performance and provide a more positive experience for students.[10] If at any point you begin to feel selfish for practicing self-care, remember that your well-being is important for your students and school as well.

## HOW STRONG IS YOUR SELF-CARE?

Most teachers I know could be practicing better self-care, but not all of us are falling apart at the seams. You might still stay late at school occasionally and not always get a full eight hours of sleep, but overall, you've found a good balance. If you fall into that category, I commend you, and I'm sure you can still find some ways in this book to improve your self-care practice. Some of you though, are no doubt close to a breakdown. Not quite sure where you fall on that spectrum? Take the following quiz to find out.

Read each statement and circle (or tally on a piece of paper)

---

9    Ingersoll, Merrill, Stuckey, and Collins, "Seven Trends."

10   U. Klussmann, et al., "Teachers' Occupational Well-Being and Quality of Instruction: The Important Role of Self-Regulatory Patterns," *Journal of Educational Psychology* 100, no. 3 (2008): 711.

## BURNOUT

Burnout is the specter of teaching, and most other helping professions too, but I have to admit I didn't know its real definition until doing research for this book. Had you asked me before, I would have said my peak burnout was during my mental breakdown in the fall of my last year of teaching. In fact, I now realize the actual period of burnout for me was the months *after* that breakdown, when I felt so disillusioned and like it was just not possible to do my job well.

So, what is the definition of burnout? The World Health Organization defines it as follows:

> "Burn-out is a syndrome conceptualized as resulting from chronic workplace stress that has not been successfully managed. It is characterized by three dimensions:
> * feelings of energy depletion or exhaustion;
> * increased mental distance from one's job, or feelings of negativism or cynicism related to one's job; and
> * reduced professional efficacy."[1]

The second bullet point perhaps explains why I got called into my assistant principal's office that spring for rolling my eyes in a team meeting in which we were told we shouldn't require any resources other than the Common Core standards for teaching language arts. Pre-burnout, my reaction might have been feelings of overwhelm and inadequacy. During burnout, my reaction was, essentially, "This is bullshit." Neither are healthy or helpful reactions.

Many of the primary risk factors for burnout involve the work environment, which we'll get into more in the vocational self-care section. Nonetheless, practicing strong self-care is also an important part of avoiding burnout. Again, if at any point you begin to feel selfish for practicing self-care, keep in mind that doing so decreases your risk of burnout, which is a worthwhile goal by anyone's standards.

---

1    World Health Organization, "Burn-out an 'Occupational Phenomenon': International Classification of Diseases," accessed November 11, 2019, http://www.who.int/mental_health/evidence/burn-out/en/.

whether that statement is true for you rarely/never, sometimes, or often. You can also take a digital version of this quiz at bit.ly/teacherselfcarequiz.

## Self-Care Assessment Quiz

| | Rarely/ Never | Sometimes | Often |
|---|---|---|---|
| I see non-work friends at least once a week. | 0 | 1 | 2 |
| I make time for my hobbies. | 0 | 1 | 2 |
| I have enough time to spend with my family. | 0 | 1 | 2 |
| I find my job satisfying. | 0 | 1 | 2 |
| I feel good about myself. | 0 | 1 | 2 |
| I get enough sleep. | 0 | 1 | 2 |
| I say no to responsibilities I don't think I can handle. | 0 | 1 | 2 |
| I exercise several times a week. | 0 | 1 | 2 |
| My job feels manageable. | 0 | 1 | 2 |
| I stay home from work when I'm sick. | 0 | 1 | 2 |
| I schedule and go to my needed medical appointments. | 0 | 1 | 2 |
| I have trouble falling asleep because I am worrying about school. | 2 | 1 | 0 |
| I stay at work more than an hour after school ends, or spend more than an hour working at home on weeknights. | 2 | 1 | 0 |
| I cry about school-related issues. | 2 | 1 | 0 |
| I do schoolwork on both Saturdays and Sundays. | 2 | 1 | 0 |
| I don't feel like I am a good enough teacher. | 2 | 1 | 0 |
| I dread going to work. | 2 | 1 | 0 |
| I feel irritable more often than I used to. | 2 | 1 | 0 |
| I'm exhausted. | 2 | 1 | 0 |
| I feel guilty when I'm not working. | 2 | 1 | 0 |

Now add up the numbers you circled to get your score and use the following chart to understand your results. I asked teachers to take this same quiz in November 2019 and have included the results below so you can see where other teachers fall in the results.

| 0-10 | 11-20 | 21-30 | 31-40 |
|---|---|---|---|
| *You are likely seriously struggling with self-care.* | *You are likely struggling with self-care.* | *You are likely practicing adequate self-care.* | *You are likely practicing strong self-care.* |
| You are having a difficult time taking care of yourself and need to make some serious changes. | You may be keeping your head above water, but barely. You need to prioritize self-care. | You know you could be practicing better self-care, but you're managing and coping adequately overall. | You get stressed out sometimes, but you're generally doing well with balancing taking care of yourself and teaching. |
| *12 percent\* of teachers scored in this range* | *57 percent\* of teachers scored in this range* | *27 percent\* of teachers scored in this range* | *4 percent\* of teachers scored in this range* |

*\*Of 195 quiz-takers in November 2019.*

This is not an official psychological screener of any kind; it's merely an inventory of indicators of self-care. Of course, you know yourself best and there are factors that a quiz like this doesn't take into account. If you scored a 25, for example, but don't feel like your self-care is truly adequate, trust yourself!

Conversely, if you scored below a 10 and feel like it's no big deal, think again: it is. Out of the 195 teachers who took this quiz, only 12 percent scored in that lowest range. I would have scored in that range myself if I had taken this quiz during my last year of teaching, so I can relate to what you may be thinking. I thought all teachers were exhausted and spent their weeknights and weekends working. Worse yet, what I think I *really* thought was that all *good* teachers were doing that. That's a lie. Being a good teacher does not mean neglecting your basic needs.

You don't need to be angry with yourself if you scored lower than you'd like. I've had several teachers message me after taking the quiz, telling me their score would have been much lower, or much higher, the year before. All teachers are not in the same situation. You are likely not even in exactly the same situation yourself from year to year. If you've been teaching first grade for fifteen years in the same classroom, hopefully you're not spending your whole weekend doing schoolwork. If you're transferred the following year to fourth grade with no team partner and no curriculum for any of the subjects, a lot more of your free time just got eaten up. But you need to take these changes into account so you can still maintain a healthy lifestyle. As a first-grade teacher, maybe you had cute craftivities for students to complete every Friday after their spelling quiz. As a new fourth-grade teacher, you should probably allow them independent reading time instead.

It's possible, however, that these kinds of changes won't be enough in some situations. Some schools and positions are just really, really not conducive to practicing strong self-care. If your school consistently requires you to work after school hours and on weekends, penalizes you for taking your sick days, allows for no maternity leave, and constantly eliminates your prep time . . . it's okay to leave. I'm reluctant to even write that, because schools with these conditions are in as much need of good teachers as other schools. But if you leave now (or, more likely, at the end of the school year) and find a school where you can thrive, you may be able to teach for years to come, rather than burning out and leaving the profession altogether. However, there are many, many aspects of self-care that *are* in your control, and I encourage you to try the suggestions in this book before you decide to leave. Even with the most understanding administration at the most well-resourced school, you can still burn out if you don't prioritize your well-being.

I originally asked teachers to take a version of the Self-Care Assessment Quiz just to make sure it wasn't too skewed one way or the other. I wanted to make sure I was neither suggesting an impossible self-care standard with the results or setting the bar too low. I didn't expect to find the results so interesting unto themselves.

In the original survey, I added a question asking how long respondents had been teaching, because I had a theory that the teachers who had been teaching longer would practice better self-care. I thought this might be the case because: (1) Teachers who hadn't practiced strong self-care might have left teaching, and (2) Teachers who had been teaching longer might be less stressed and have a smaller workload, thus with more time to practice self-care. I wanted to be able to reassure newer teachers that it gets better.

This was a nice theory, but alas, the results don't support it. Every group of teachers—first-year teachers and those who had been teaching two to five years, six to ten years, and more than eleven years, respectively—had an average score in the "struggling with self-care" range. For first- and second-through fifth-year teachers, the average score was 16, and for sixth- through tenth-year teachers and teachers who had been teaching for eleven or more years, the average score was 18. Unfortunately, it does not seem that self-care practice is likely to just naturally get stronger over time.

Forty-six percent of teachers who took this quiz indicated that they sometimes feel like they're not a good enough teacher. Forty-one percent said they often feel that way. Out of all the results of this quiz, that one breaks my heart the most, because I've worked in schools and gotten to know thousands of teachers through The Designer Teacher and Teacher Care Crate. And while I know we all have room for improvement in our teaching practice—and we all know one or two teachers in our school who genuinely don't seem like they're in the right profession—41 percent of us should not frequently think we're not good enough. *You are good enough.*

Only 1 percent of teachers reported that they're rarely or never exhausted. And while 26 percent said they're sometimes exhausted, in a result that will surprise not a single teacher, 73 percent said they're often exhausted. These numbers do not add up, my friends! Eighty-seven percent of us sometimes or often feel we're not good enough teachers. And yet 97 percent are sometimes or often exhausted. Seventy-six percent of us sometimes or often cry about work. It's clear that most teachers put an incredible amount of effort and emotional energy into their work. It's devastating to discover that despite this, many, if not most, teachers sometimes or often feel they're not good enough.

In less depressing news, 48 percent of teachers who took this quiz often find their jobs satisfying, and 47 percent sometimes do. Only 5 percent rarely or never find it satisfying. I'm pretty confident that not too many other careers can boast those numbers.

So take heart. Teaching may be a hard job, but it's a rewarding one. And it's important enough that it's worth the effort of adjusting your mindset and your actions so that this job can be a sustainable one.

## ACTS OF SELF-CARE

If you're not sure where to start with incorporating self-care into your life, read this list and circle or highlight a few activities you would like (or need) to try. I've organized these ideas by the amount of time they usually take, with free or inexpensive ideas at the top, and those that are more of a splurge or investment toward the bottom.

| 5 Minutes or Less | 1 Hour or Less | Longer than 1 Hour |
|---|---|---|
| × Take a deep breath | × Go for a walk | × Hang out with a friend |
| × Say an affirmation | × Go to bed early | × Have a work-free evening |
| × Cuddle with a pet | × Journal | × Organize a space in your home |
| × Stretch | × Read for pleasure | × Go to a needed doctor's appointment |
| × Drink water | × Meditate | × Take a mental health day |
| × Express gratitude | × Go for a bike ride | × Sleep in |
| × Dance | × Practice a hobby | × Visit a museum |
| × Take your meds | × Take a bath | × Take yourself out to a meal |
| × Look at a photo of someone or something you love | × Have a work-free lunch | × Get your hair cut |
| × Listen to music | × Take a nap | × Attend an event |
| × Wear something you love | × Call someone you love | × Go hiking |
| × Write down three things that went well today or yesterday | × Draw, color, or paint | × Movie night |
| × Have a cup of tea | × Pack a healthy lunch | × Have a date night with your partner |
| × Light a candle | × Garden | × Visit a day spa |
| × Pick or buy yourself flowers | × Make a collage | × Go on a day trip |
| × Apply a face mask | × Practice yoga | × Go on a vacation |
| | × Soak your feet | |
| | × Go to the library | |
| | × Exercise | |
| | × Enjoy nature | |
| | × Go to a coffee shop | |
| | × Work on a puzzle | |
| | × Therapy | |
| | × Get a massage | |

We will get into the specific forms of self-care and ideas for practicing each shortly, but this list is great to refer to when you know you need to do something to take better care of yourself.

## Self-Care Calendar

Believe it or not, you deserve to do something for yourself every single day! One of the best ways to ensure you do this is to make a self-care calendar. Be realistic about what you can do.

Here's a sample of my school week self-care schedule:

| Monday | Tuesday | Wednesday |
|---|---|---|
| × Morning Affirmations<br>× Therapy | × Morning Affirmations<br>× Afternoon Puzzle Time (30 min.) | × Morning Affirmations<br>× Evening Yoga |

| Thursday | Friday |
|---|---|
| × Morning Affirmations<br>× Afternoon Puzzle Time (30 min.) | × Morning Affirmations<br>× Evening Yoga |

| Saturday | Sunday |
|---|---|
| × Morning Puzzle Time | × Meal Prep<br>× Evening Bath |

I didn't start out doing all these things when I first began practicing self-care. I began with yoga once a week, and eventually added a second class. I used to only puzzle or do another calming activity for ten minutes, and then gradually extended it to thirty. Try adding new activities slowly as you figure out what works for you.

Of course, many acts of self-care should be done every day and don't need to be added to a schedule, like taking your medications, drinking enough water, and getting enough sleep.

It may feel silly or indulgent to make a schedule for self-care, but, especially if you're routine-oriented like me, it can be really helpful! On any given Sunday night, I don't feel like I have time to take a relaxing bath. But if I plan on it, I prioritize working efficiently to ensure I wrap up my work by 8 or 8:30

p.m. so I have time. The same goes for an exercise class or just about any other self-care activity.

You can make a preliminary self-care schedule now, or you may want to wait until you've read through the rest of this book to collect some ideas.

## MAKING TIME FOR SELF-CARE

It's one thing to list self-care ideas and insist that you should implement them, but I know very well that a real or perceived lack of time is a teacher's biggest challenge when it comes to practicing self-care.

To make time for self-care, you must first acknowledge you can't do it all. Teaching is a job that is really at least two jobs, probably a bit more. Once you realize you can't do everything, you can let go of that goal. I know from experience that it's not as simple as "work less" or "stop bringing work home." What we do matters, and that's what makes it so rewarding—but also so hard to set boundaries. So, it's not a matter of what doesn't matter, but what matters *less*. What's taking up too much of your time or causing you stress? What can you cross off? Which tasks can you delegate?

After my mental breakdown, I stopped laminating. I don't even hate laminating; trapping something forever between two pieces of plastic is kind of satisfying, plus you can listen to a podcast while you do it. But it was eating up time. It wasn't essential, so it went. Turns out centers can still be completed unlaminated. You can still hang up a poster unlaminated. We laminate to preserve, but not everything is worth preserving. Unless you're positive you'll still be using the resource in five years' time, skip the lamination. It's terrible for the earth anyway. And if it turns out you do need it after it falls apart . . . guess what? You can reprint it! I'm pretty sure using two pieces of paper is better for the environment than one piece of paper and one plastic sleeve anyway. So, what's *your* laminating? Maybe it's actually laminating, like it was for me. Maybe it's prizes. Maybe it's the extra committee you're on. It sucks not doing something you feel you're supposed to do, or something that's helping kids. But you need to be a bit ruthless for the sake of your own well-being, and in turn, that of your students.

*What are you giving up by working all the time?* My therapist asked me this question during one of our first few sessions. I paused. I was a little embarrassed by my answer, but what I truly missed doing on nights I was too busy working was watching a TV show with my husband. Around 8:30 he would hopefully look up and ask if we were watching a show, and 90 percent of the time I would helplessly say I just couldn't. There's no reason why a healthy twenty-six-year-old with only one job and no children shouldn't be able to take a half hour out of her night to watch a TV show with her husband. I encourage you to ask yourself this same question. What are you giving up? Maybe it's time with your spouse or your kids. Maybe it's a hobby you're passionate about. Whenever you're about to run one more center through the laminator, remember that thing you're giving up.

Laminating may not be the task you need to give up in your workload, but chances are there are other tasks where you can make changes to save yourself some much-needed time. Here are a few ideas of what to spend less time on or eliminate completely:

× **Changing out bulletin board paper and borders.** Use neutral fabric or fadeless paper for the background and borders that aren't seasonal. Put them up at the beginning of the year and don't change them for the rest of the year. Re-staple those borders as needed.

× **Grading.** Have students check each other's work when possible. Narrow what you grade down to what's truly necessary. You don't have to grade every worksheet, I promise.

× **Making elaborate anchor charts.** The most effective anchor chart is written neatly and clearly, and created at least partially with students. If it's a chart that will only be needed for one day, consider creating and displaying it digitally.

× **Creating all your own materials.** What and how you teach certainly depends on your specific students, but don't feel pressured to recreate the wheel! Make use of the resources available at your school, or find comprehensive resources online that will save you a significant amount of time.

× **Making paper copies.** If you're lucky enough to have devices with internet access for your students, make full use of them! Many passages, worksheets, and quizzes can be distributed using Google Classroom or similar programs. It may take some time initially to switch over to a new system, but ultimately it will save you tons of time and frustration at the copy machine. If you don't have a full set of classroom devices, you can still make use of what you do have by having the students work in shifts. For example, while half of the class is taking a quiz on the tablets, the other half could be picking out books in your classroom library. When time is up, the groups switch.

× **Running an extracurricular.** I appreciate the teachers who run sports and clubs. I don't want to discourage you from doing so if it's something you're passionate about and it makes a meaningful difference for kids. But if you feel like you don't have the time to practice self-care, don't take on extra responsibilities. Take care of yourself first.

- ✗ **Giving out homework.** Unless your school requires it, consider eliminating homework. Research is mixed about whether it boosts achievement, especially for students in elementary school.[11] You'll not only save time by not having to come up with the homework, but by not having to copy, distribute, or grade it.

- ✗ **Creating classroom transformations and themes.** These are all over social media, and they do look super fun! But your students are better off having a well-rested, happy teacher than a burnt-out teacher and a room that looks like a rainforest. Promise.

- ✗ **Filling all your walls.** If your walls have tons of bulletin boards, you may feel like you need to fill them. But a classroom covered from floor to ceiling with decorations, or even learning materials, can be overstimulating for students. Try covering these bulletin boards with a plain colored fabric or paper at the beginning of the year, and then add to them only as needed.

- ✗ **Maintaining a prize box.** I just like giving people things, which was the main reason I had a prize box for my first few years of teaching. But, like laminating, it was a task that ate into my precious personal time. When I eliminated it, there were a few complaints, but the students forgot about it soon enough!

- ✗ **Writing weekly newsletters.** If creating a newsletter doesn't take you much time and you find that parents are making use of it, great! If you notice parents rarely read it, try moving to monthly newsletters or moving it online. There's no reason to continue a task that isn't useful.

---

11   Natalie Wexler, "Why Homework Doesn't Seem to Boost Learning—And How It Could," *Forbes*, January 3, 2019, https://www.forbes.com/sites/nataliewexler/2019/01/03/why-homework-doesnt-seem-to-boost-learning-and-how-it-could/.

× **Giving out gifts.** Gift giving is my love language, and I loved giving my little group of resource students gifts on holidays. Granted, that was usually fewer than ten students—not the thirty-plus that many general education teachers have! You are under no obligation to give students gifts for every (or any) holiday, no matter what you may see on social media.

Many tasks can't be eliminated from your workload, but here are a few ways to manage your time and certain tasks more efficiently:

× **Create templates.** Use templates for documents you have to create over and over again. For example, as a special education teacher, I made an IEP template in a Google Doc, and duplicated it whenever I needed to write a new IEP. While IEPs shouldn't be entirely fill-in-the-blank, you'll still save time by having the outline written and only having to change a few things in certain sections, like test scores.

× **Time yourself.** Allot yourself a certain amount of time to work on a given task, and then stick to it. Unless the time you've allotted is wildly unreasonable, you'll find you're usually able to work within your time limit.

× **When you're working, work.** One way to ensure that a task drags on all evening is to check your phone every five minutes or watch TV while you're trying to complete it. Instead, plan in breaks and a set an end time when you can fully relax. I use the Pomodoro Technique, a time-management method developed by Francesco Cirillo. It consists of working steadily for twenty-five minutes at a time, with five-minute breaks between work segments. After you complete four twenty-five-minute segments (called pomodoros, after the tomato-shaped timer Cirillo used), you take a longer break. This method works well for me because twenty-five minutes is such a reasonable amount of time. I don't get such an urge to check my phone or email when I know I don't have to wait that long.

× **Assign students meaningful jobs.** While some tasks are made harder by having students do them, there are many jobs you can give your students that will lighten your own load. Sharpening pencils, checking that devices are plugged in, distributing graded work, sweeping, and wiping desks are all jobs many students can handle. With older students, you may even be able to hand off tasks like organizing the classroom library and changing the date on the board.

## *Part 2:*

# TYPES OF SELF-CARE

As a teacher, you likely know you need to take better care of yourself. You may have some ideas about what that means—eating better or sleeping more, for example—but you may not have thought about the full range of what self-care includes. For the purposes of this guide, I've divided the kinds of self-care into seven categories: physical, emotional, spiritual, social, intellectual, vocational, and environmental.

### PHYSICAL SELF-CARE

While teaching may feel like a job that is mostly of the heart and mind, our physical bodies are what allow us to do the job at all. While perhaps less physical a vocation than, say, being a professional athlete, teaching still requires that we take care of our bodies, and doing so allows us to both feel better and perform better. Physical self-care covers a broad range of activities, so I've further divided this area of self-care into seven sub-categories: medical, sick days, grooming, clothing, exercise, nutrition, and sleep.

### Medical

If you ask a group of teachers when the last time was they went to the dentist, the answers are truly alarming. Six months, people! You're supposed to go to the dentist every six months! Make a list of all the appointments you need to maintain your physical well-being, and record the last appointment you had. Searching the calendar on your phone is helpful for this! Consider adding a page to your planner or journal with a chart like the one below. If you're overdue, make the next appointment.

| APPOINTMENT TYPE | HOW OFTEN YOU SHOULD GO | LAST APPT. | NEXT APPT. |
|---|---|---|---|
| General Doctor | Yearly | | |
| Dentist | Every six months | | |
| Gynecologist | Yearly | | |
| Psychiatrist | | | |
| Dermatologist | | | |
| Ophthalmologist | | | |
| Allergist | | | |
| Physical Therapist | | | |
| | | | |

Try to schedule yearly and twice yearly appointments over summer and winter break. For appointments you need to make more frequently, try to find a provider that is open evenings or weekends. Four o'clock in the afternoon is a great appointment time that most teachers can make, but other professionals can't, so it's often open. While at your current appointment, make your next appointment. I avoided this for years because I never know what my schedule will look like in six months or a year, but if you do this, you at least have it on the books. Even if you have to reschedule, it's a reminder to make and go to the appointment.

In addition to appointments, many of us have daily medications we should be taking. I can't recommend a weekly pill organizer enough! It may make you feel like a senior citizen, but it will also keep you from ever wondering whether you took your meds or not. You can see quite clearly whether the day's compartment is empty or full. I've been taking anxiety medicine every night for seven years, and it can be difficult sometimes to know whether I'm remembering taking them that night or the night before, despite having an alarm on my phone reminding me to take them. And an SSRI *really* isn't something you can safely skip, and it's not something you want to take a double dose of either. Enter my pill organizer! I haven't missed or questioned a single dose since I got it, and it's had the added bonus of ensuring I take my allergy medication and vitamins as well.

## Sick Days

While we're talking about medical self-care, USE YOUR SICK DAYS. This can be a divisive topic for teachers. I was at a conference once where the keynote speaker asked those teachers with ten or more sick days saved to raise their hands. A sea of hands went up. He said to keep your hand up if you had more than fifteen . . .more than twenty . . . more than thirty . . . more than fifty. He kept going until only one person's hand remained up. "How many sick days have you banked?" he asked the woman. The answer was 327.

Whenever I remind teachers to use their sick days on social media, I get a TON of comments telling me about truly terrible situations at their schools. Many, many teachers in the United States get zero days of maternity leave, and are forced to hoard sick days to have any time at home with a new baby. Others have told me they will get docked on evaluations for taking more than a certain number, even though they are legally entitled to those days. I think both these situations are appalling. That said, I know plenty of teachers with more sick days stored than they can ever use. Some teachers seem to take a perverse pride in having an enormous number of sick days stored. In my research for this book, I even came across a study that tried to measure teacher effectiveness by how *few* days off teachers took.

Insisting on going to work when you're sick or exhausted, day after day, year after year, is not healthy behavior. It does not make you a better teacher or a morally superior person. I see so many teacher memes floating around stating that it's easier to go to school sick than it is to make sub plans. That's . . . not true. And it's not modeling healthy behavior for our students. I know we wouldn't want them to come to school sick, and we complain when they do. So why are we doing it ourselves?

One day during my second year of teaching, I woke up with horrible menstrual cramps. It was so bad I was almost crying. But I wasn't going to stay home for cramps, right? So after popping a few ibuprofens, I headed to school even though I felt lightheaded. As I was getting ready for the day in my classroom, I collapsed and passed out from the pain. Someone found me and called the principal. I was mortified to wake up and find myself on the floor with people staring down at me. The nurse took my blood pressure and said it was too low to let me drive home, so I had to have someone come pick me up. I might have once heard this story and thought it showed dedication, but now I just think it shows foolishness. I'm thankful I didn't pass out in front of students—they don't need to see their teacher lying on the floor!

Unfortunately, that was not the only day I was sent home from school. We have to take responsibility for our own health and know when we shouldn't go to work. You are not so important that the school won't keep running without you for one day.

If you're a parent or are planning on becoming one in a school or district without maternity leave, I'm sorry. I know it is not within everyone's power to do so, but consider finding a new district with better benefits, and be sure to let your school know why you're leaving. Poor working conditions don't improve if everyone just continues to put up with them. I'm not exactly shocked to find that many areas are now facing a teacher shortage. While I feel for the students and other teachers affected, I hope this shortage is a wake-up call for districts and politicians. Teachers take care of other people's children all day, and they deserve to be able to care for their own as well.

If your school docks you evaluation points for using sick days, dig a little deeper and find out if this is actually policy. If you are represented by a union, you might discover that it's against your union contract to dock points for sick days. If that's the case, make sure you let your administration know this with your union representative present. If there truly is a policy in place that penalizes teachers for taking sick days, advocate for change or consider leaving your district. That may seem extreme, but when we continue to work for schools that treat us unfairly without complaint, we encourage them to continue doing so. A teacher in New Mexico actually filed a class-action lawsuit against the New Mexico Public Education Department in 2017 for penalizing teachers for taking more than six days of sick leave, even when they are allowed to do so in their contract.[12]

If you're not saving up for maternity leave and you don't live in a district that penalizes you for taking your sick days, but you *still* find it hard to take a day, here are a few tips to make it easier:

- Prepare for days off now. Sub plans getting you down? You can find full-day sub plans on sites like Teachers Pay Teachers for just about any grade. If making sub plans is what keeps you from taking days off, purchase a set now

12 Rick Nathanson, "Lawsuit Filed over Sick Leave Policy for NM Teachers," *Las Cruces Sun-News*, April 17, 2017, https://www.lcsun-news.com/story/news/education/2017/04/17/lawsuit-filed-over-sick-leave-policy-nm-teachers/100565664/.

and prepare it ahead of time. Then, when you need to take a day, it's ready!

* Decide now what merits taking a sick day. My firm rule is that if I have a fever, am throwing up, can't speak (this happens to me strangely often!), or have a severe allergic reaction, I'm staying home. Tell your partner or a friend and have them hold you accountable. I can't tell you the number of times my husband insisted I stay home, and I'm grateful for it.

* I absolutely understand wanting to have some sick days on reserve for emergencies. Decide now how many you want to save, and at what point you will use them. For example, if you have eight days this year, perhaps you won't take any mental health days until October or November, if you haven't had to use them for another reason. If it reaches April and you have five or more left, you'll take another one. This will keep you on track for not hoarding those days!

You're entitled to your sick and personal days. If you don't take them, you're essentially working those days for free. Teachers are professionals and deserve to be paid for their work.

## Grooming

When you hear about self-care, especially on social media, it's often in the context of grooming and beauty. Manicures, face masks, and bubble baths are great if you enjoy them, but keep in mind that we hear and see the most about grooming and beauty only because it's the most marketable kind of self-care. This category has a vast range and is going to look different for everyone. Much of it is optional. However, if you begin neglecting the basics, that can be a sign of depression.

Here's what I consider the basics:

* Brushing teeth twice a day
* Showering at least every forty-eight hours
* Cleansing your face and hair as appropriate for your skin and hair type
* Wearing clean, neat clothes to school that fit your dress code

Just about everything else is optional, even if it sometimes feels mandatory, especially for women. Consider the tasks on the following list and whether they are things you do for yourself or are an extra burden. Do they make you feel good or do you find them annoying? The answers will be different for everyone, and that's fine!

* Wearing makeup
* Painting your nails
* Hair removal, such as shaving or waxing
* Dressing fashionably
* Straightening or curling your hair
* Elaborate skincare routines
* Wearing contacts instead of glasses

I recently stopped tweezing and waxing my eyebrows and realized my brows look totally fine left alone. On the other hand, I like taking good care of my curly hair and getting it cut every few months to keep it a nice shape. I love dressing up and putting together outfits, but my makeup these days is minimal at best. This part of self-care is about doing what makes *you* feel your best. If you hate leaving the house without lipstick, make time for it in the morning. If putting on makeup is a chore for you, skip it. As long as you look professional and feel comfortable, you're good to go!

**Clothing**

My first year of teaching, I hastily bought some black dress pants and a few tops to wear with them. The pants were cropped, which meant that once winter hit, I was wearing an awkward combo of socks that would cover my bare ankles with flats. It wasn't that big of a deal, but it was something that irked me and felt a little bit not-right all winter long. I was short on funds (hello, first-year teacher!), but I wish I would've just skimped on something else and bought some dang full-length pants!

Wearing clothes you love and feel comfortable in can make you feel more relaxed and prepared. This doesn't have to mean buying a whole new wardrobe—in fact, it usually means the opposite! I'll mention it throughout this book, but reading and following *The Life-Changing Magic of Tidying Up* by Marie Kondo is a GREAT way to streamline your wardrobe and your life. Keep and wear only the clothes you love, even if that reduces your wardrobe significantly. Yes, your students may comment on your repeating outfits but, let's be honest, they do that anyway. (They're all DIFFERENT striped shirts, OKAY?!)

Consider what will make your day at school easier and more comfortable. Here are a few ideas to get you started:

- If you have to bend down or sit on the floor a lot, consider wearing at least knee-length skirts and dresses so you don't have to worry about your hemline.
- If your building has fluctuating temperatures, dress in layers and keep a neutral sweater at school.
- Consider investing in one or two pairs of really good shoes with support. Flats from Target do not count! So many teachers get plantar fasciitis, so it's a worthwhile investment. There are so many cute supportive shoes out there that you won't even need to look like your grandmother in her orthopedic sneakers.

* If you find picking out outfits stressful, try putting together a capsule wardrobe. You can find tons of information and examples online, but the idea is to put together a mini collection of clothes that all go together and then wear only these items for a certain amount of time.

* If you feel like you never have anything to wear or struggle with putting together outfits, try an outfit-building app like Cladwell. You can add all your regularly worn clothes to the app, and it shows you all possible outfit combinations. This is particularly helpful if you want to try a capsule wardrobe.

* Plan your outfits for the week on Sunday. In my experience, 6 a.m. is the absolute worst time to try to pick out what to wear. Choose your outfits ahead of time so you can just put them on and go.

* Stop buying clothes that need ironing or dry cleaning. I line dry almost all my clothes, but that's about as far as I'll go with upkeep. Unless you find yourself with excess time (which is doubtful, since you're reading this book!), why would you spend time ironing or dropping off dry cleaning?!

* Wear an apron or fanny pack. As a special education teacher traveling from room to room, I quickly started wearing a half apron. It gave me a secure place to stow my classroom keys, pens, stickers, and anything else I would need throughout the day. Wearing one also makes clothes without pockets less bothersome!

If you love expressing yourself through creative outfits, go for it! Just don't let clothes take up your precious time if fashion isn't something you enjoy.

## Exercise

Many of us have a negative relationship with exercise, whether it's due to attempted weight loss, injuries, or childhood traumatization in gym class. Ultimately, though, we need to move our bodies to be healthy and to feel good. I don't think you need me to list all the benefits of regular exercise, but know that it's also an important part of self-care. Exercise does NOT have to look like getting up at 5 a.m. every day to hit the gym before school. It doesn't have to mean training for a marathon or playing a team sport, though it can! Find something that fits into your lifestyle and that you enjoy, so you'll actually do it.

For my first several years of teaching, I was usually training for a race of some kind. It was beneficial in that I followed a pretty strict training schedule, which meant I was exercising at least four times a week. Ultimately, though, it became just another task on my to-do list, and it took up way too much time for me to want to keep up with it consistently. The key is to find something you can keep up with, and for me, running wasn't it.

Instead, kundalini yoga (a meditation-based form of yoga that still incorporates exercise) twice a week has been an amazing form of self-care for me, both physically and spiritually. I started going every week on Friday evenings at 5:30, and it was the perfect way to transition myself from school mode into the weekend. Now I have a monthly membership and go twice a week, and I also try to participate in events and workshops held at the studio. Initially, it still felt a tiny bit like work to get myself together to go to yoga, but now I absolutely crave it. I don't feel guilty for going and not working, because it's built into my schedule. If I'm traveling or can't go due to an emergency, I really miss it. If you haven't traditionally had a good relationship with exercise or don't consider yourself athletic, you might want to check out kundalini yoga! Challenging yourself physically is absolutely a part of it, but you'll find that you can always rest or modify postures as needed. In my experience, the kundalini community is very welcoming and accepting of all ages, genders, and body types.

If you already have an exercise routine that works for you, great! Stick with it. If not, read through the list below and pick one or more to try.

* Yoga—don't forget that there are many types of yoga, so don't give up if you don't like the first form you try
* Running
* Walking
* Hiking
* Climbing
* Dancing—look for a class for a dance form you've always wanted to try, like salsa, tap, or Irish step dancing
* Swimming
* Biking
* Weight lifting
* Elliptical or other exercise machines
* At-home workouts (there are a TON on YouTube!)
* Fitness classes
* Team sports—most cities have adult sports teams, so try searching for something you played in high school or have always wanted to try

Look for something that makes you feel GOOD. If going to the gym doesn't do that for you, that's fine. There are lots of other kinds of exercise to try, and many have the added benefit of belonging to a community as well.

I often see teachers following strict fitness programs that involve daily cardio workouts and drinking some kind of shake. Followers of these programs always seem super enthusiastic at the beginning, but if you're considering one, make sure you think about whether it's sustainable for you. I might muster the energy to follow one of these programs for a few weeks, but I know very well I'm not going to follow one for the rest of my life or even a year. The best form of exercise is the one that you can do consistently.

Once you've found something you like, make it a part of your schedule. If you're like me, you may never feel you have time to exercise. So give it a standing appointment in your life. My yoga classes are in my Google Calendar, even though I have a monthly membership and could go or not go to as many classes as I want. Like any habit, accountability is beneficial. Let a friend or partner know when you plan to exercise and ask them to follow up with you. You can even exercise together!

Aside from "official" exercise, there are plenty of other ways to incorporate physical activity into your daily life. As Michelle Segar, author and sustainable behavior change scientist says, "all movement counts."[13] Many people seem to think that only sweaty workouts count as exercise. But in fact, researchers measure physical activity using a unit called a MET (metabolic equivalent), and you can double your METs just by getting up and walking across the room. Three METs or more qualifies as moderate activity, and lots of everyday activities will get you to three METs, such as climbing stairs or even vigorous vacuuming![14] So don't think that just because you can't make it to the gym on a given day that there's no way to get any exercise.

Here are a few ways you can increase your movement that don't involve setting aside any special time or using any specific equipment:

13   Maria Godoy, "From Couch Potato to Fitness Buff: How I Learned to Love Exercise," NPR.org, January 14, 2019, https://www.npr.org/sections/health-shots/2019/01/14/684118974/from-couch-potato-to-fitness-buff-how-i-learned-to-love-exercise.

14   Godoy, "From Couch Potato to Fitness Buff."

× Join your students on a movement break.

× Take the stairs instead of the elevator.

× Walk around the room to work with students instead of having them come to you.

× Stand or walk while teaching instead of sitting.

× Join your students for part of outdoor recess or gym class.

× Walk or bike to work if possible. If that seems too intimidating or time-consuming, consider doing so just once or twice a week.

× Clean up your classroom.

× Make your bed and put away your clothes.

All these things might seem pointless, or may even be things you actively avoid, but the truth is that just these small activities could help you multiply your daily physical activity. While living in a third-floor walkup, I was always amazed at how visitors would be huffing and puffing when they reached the third floor. I don't consider myself particularly athletic or strong, but from just walking up and down the stairs throughout the day, I could easily dash up and down them without becoming out of breath. When we moved into our current house, I kept this in mind when considering where to put my office. Despite being a bit of a trek from the first floor, I decided to put my home office in the finished attic. When I check my health stats on my phone, I can see that I average about fifteen flights of stairs a day! So if your classroom is on an upper floor, consider it a blessing in disguise.

My friend Ashley Vongphakdy, who goes by Teaching with Ashley online, started running a mile every day a few years ago, and she recently reached her 1,000th day of running! Here's her story in her own words:

*Five years into my teaching career I was exhausted and burnt out. Having always considered myself an athlete, I found myself unrecognizable. I was physically, mentally, and emotionally drained. Fitting physical activity into my day seemed impossible, unless I counted squatting down to my second graders' level. My coworker invited me to do a 100-day running challenge with other teachers. This meant we would run at least one mile every day for 100 days straight. Though we never ran together, we all understood the difficulty that came with wanting to exercise daily and the exhaustion that comes with our profession. The first few months of establishing this new habit were exhausting. I relied on my running buddies' messages of encouragement to get through each mile. After hitting 100 days of running, I kept going. I hit other mile markers: 200 days, one year, two years, and most recently 1,000 days of running. Now I can't stop and it's not because I enjoy running. It's because I enjoy taking care of myself. My physical health has improved since I began my running journey. I have more energy and haven't been sick as often. Running has helped my mental health as well. I practice mindfulness techniques while running, such as noticing how it feels when my feet hit the pavement and imagining all the hardships from the day falling off me and onto the trail. When I run, I am choosing to spend my time on just me. Those miles have carried me through some wonderful and incredibly difficult moments in my life. Running has helped me learn how to take care of myself again. Find something to do for yourself each day, whether it's morning stretches, taking a long walk, or yoga. I'm not saying to go run a mile every day. Go and show yourself some love each day because you deserve it.*

I find Ashley's story inspiring for many reasons, but mostly because she's managed to be so consistent. Exercise doesn't need to be incredibly difficult, time-consuming, or expensive. It just needs to be something you can do regularly!

### Nutrition

Like exercise, eating and nutrition can be a fraught topic. But, again like exercise, eating well and nourishing your body are important aspects of self-care. Personally, when I'm stressed I tend not to eat or try to make myself feel better by eating sugar. Neither of these things helps you feel any less stressed! Some school environments can also make eating well difficult. At my past school, it seemed like every single teacher drank multiple diet sodas a day. If there was a sugary treat in the teachers' lounge, you better believe I was stopping by several times a day to snack! We're just doing what we believe we need to do to get through the day. It's a good impulse—treating ourselves well. But ultimately we're not treating ourselves well at all when we're doing something that harms us. I asked Cole Yaverbaum, a teacher who's passionate about making healthy eating practical for teachers, to share some of her experience and a few tips. Here's what she had to say:

> When I'm hungry, I automatically get a headache. When I get a headache, I'm super grouchy. For my first two years of teaching, I really under-prioritized eating (let alone healthy eating), even though I should have known myself well enough to know that teaching with a massive headache was a horrible idea. In my third year, I recommitted to my health as a priority. While there are SO many things that are hard about teaching, having a headache because you haven't properly eaten or hydrated should not be one of them. Here are my favorite tips for health as a teacher:

*1. **Water first thing every morning.** You'll have enough time to pee it out before the school day starts and will make sure you're starting your day hydrated. Water flushes out toxins, gets your metabolism revved up for the day, and helps you make good choices about food (sometimes we think we're hungry but we're actually just so dang thirsty).*

*2. **Eat breakfast.** I don't care what it is. Put food in your body in the morning so you don't get mad at kids when you're actually just hungry. (Once you have the breakfast routine down, see if you can up your game by prioritizing healthy fats in your breakfast.)*

*3. **Don't put so much pressure on every meal**—aka eat snacks so you're not hangry by every mealtime. Stock your classroom with things you love (nuts, dark chocolate, popcorn, granola bars, crackers, and nut butter are some of my go-tos).*

*4. **Take a probiotic.** They give you good bacteria to keep your gut healthy and since about 80 percent of our immune system is located in our gut, this is a really easy way to keep your gut happy.*

*You can find more from Cole on Instagram @cookbookish_ and @ladiestalkingaboutmoney.*

I'm not a nutritionist, and there's plenty of information out there about how to eat in a healthy way, so in addition to Cole's tips, I'll just share a few things that have worked for me:

× **Meal prep.** I'm not nearly as serious about it as some people, but I make a big batch of healthy soup or another packable meal on Sunday, and then divide it up into containers to take with me each weekday. This guarantees you have a healthy lunch every day of the week without cutting into your precious evening time or rushed mornings.

- *Alternative healthy options:* If you just can't get on board the meal prep train, there are still healthy options. One of my former co-teachers ate a peanut butter and jelly sandwich on white bread every single day. That might kind of fill you up, but you're not getting much in the way of actual nutrition. If you're lucky enough to live by a Trader Joe's, they have tons of frozen lunch options, some of which are pretty good and have legitimate vegetables in them. Canned or boxed soup is another option, but just watch the sodium!

× **Consider home meal kits.** For dinners, I've had good experiences with using home meal kits. These can get pricey, but it's worth looking into to see if there's an option that fits your dietary needs and budget if you have trouble finding time to meal plan or grocery shop.

- *Alternative healthy options:* If you find yourself needing to eat out or get takeout a lot, gather some healthy, or relatively healthy, options. A burrito bowl or Mediterranean food is better for you than a burger or pizza!

× **Watch the sugar.** Coffee is a BIG part of teacher culture. Which is fine! Studies have shown a cup of coffee a day can even be good for you. But, y'all, it's the SUGAR that teachers mainline through their coffee that gets me. The recommended daily intake of sugar for women is 25 grams or fewer. A Starbucks caramel macchiato has 33 grams.

A pumpkin spice latte with whipped cream has a whopping 50 grams. So if you're stopping at Starbucks before school, you could be drinking DOUBLE the amount of recommended sugar before your day even starts. Artificial sugar isn't much better for you (possibly even worse). So do yourself a favor and cut back on the sugar in your coffee or just cut it out completely. I did this a couple years ago as a New Year's resolution, and you don't even want it anymore after a few weeks.

× **Hydrate.** While we're talking beverages, drink your water! As Cole recommended, drinking water in the morning ensures you start your day hydrated. However, there's no evidence that the average person needs to drink a gallon of plain water a day, which is something I see all the time around teacher Instagram. The National Academy of Sciences recommends 91 ounces of water a day for women, but that's your *total* intake, which includes non-water beverages (even caffeinated ones!), and 20 percent of that 91 ounces generally comes from food. So, minus the 20 percent you're getting from food, most women should be drinking around 72 ounces of liquid in some form every day. Subtract the 16 ounces you're probably having in coffee or tea form, and you're at around 56 ounces, which is infinitely more doable than a gallon. For men, the recommendation is 125 ounces, but again, that is the total for *all* water intake, not just plain water.[15] Get a reusable water bottle (I like using a glass tumbler with a straw) and keep it nearby. Having trouble finding time

---

15   The National Academies of Sciences, Engineering, and Medicine, "Report Sets Dietary Intake Levels for Water, Salt, and Potassium to Maintain Health and Reduce Chronic Disease Risk," news release, February 11, 2004, https://www.nationalacademies.org/news/2004/02/report-sets-dietary-intake-levels-for-water-salt-and-potassium-to-maintain-health-and-reduce-chronic-disease-risk.

to use the restroom to keep up with your water intake? Try working a bathroom break into your schedule. Do you have a co-teacher, aide, or other adult in your room at any point in the day? Try scheduling a mutually agreed upon time when you know you can head out for a quick bathroom break. As a special education teacher, I covered classes like this frequently and never minded. Of course, be sure to return the favor!

× **Eat breakfast.** I second Cole's tip to have breakfast. I've never been one to start frying up eggs before work at 6 a.m., but do make sure you're eating something that will fuel you until lunch! Personally, I make my own sugarless granola in a big batch every two weeks or so and eat it with Greek yogurt and berries. Smoothies with plenty of fruits and veggies are a good option as well, if you need something you can eat on the go.

× **Take your vitamins.** In general, it's best to get your vitamins and minerals from your diet, but multivitamins do still have proven benefits, especially for women of childbearing age.[16] Make sure yours has folic acid and iron. As much as it pains me to eat the extra sugar, I've found that gummy vitamins work best for me.

The idea of eating healthy can feel overwhelming if it's not something you've been prioritizing. If this is true for you, know that you don't have to change everything at once. Start with just one thing, like drinking more water, and once it's become

---

16    Johns Hopkins Medicine, "Is There Really Any Benefit to Multivitamins?," The Johns Hopkins University, The Johns Hopkins Hospital, and Johns Hopkins Health System, accessed November 7, 2019, www.hopkinsmedicine.org/health/wellness-and-prevention/is-there-really-any-benefit-to-multivitamins.

a habit, move on to other areas of your nutrition that need improvement.

## Sleep

Lack of quality sleep makes every bad situation worse. You have less energy, less patience, and are just an all-around less pleasant person. Teachers who don't get enough sleep report more mood swings and health problems.[17] And yet, even though it hurts both health and job performance, teachers seem to find it incredibly hard to prioritize sleep.

According to Centers for Disease Control and Prevention (CDC), adults aged eighteen to sixty need seven or more hours of sleep a night. One study found that 43 percent of teachers sleep less than six hours a night![18] Frankly, I don't know how they're functioning. I guess the answer is, many teachers are *not* adequately functioning. The same study found that 25 percent of teachers reported that sleepiness impaired their daily activities.

Work backward from the time you get up to the time you need to go to sleep in order to get at least seven hours of sleep, and kind in mind that seven hours is the MINIMUM. You may need more to be adequately rested—I know I certainly do! Set yourself a bedtime, and do your best to stick to it.

My husband said to me a long time ago, "If you're tired, the best thing you can do is sleep," and I remember getting so annoyed. How nice it must be to just sleep whenever you're tired! But he had a point. If you're exhausted, you're not functioning at your best.

---

17   Denise H. Amschler and James F. McKenzie, "Perceived Sleepiness, Sleep Habits and Sleep Concerns of Public School Teachers, Administrators and Other Personnel," *American Journal of Health Education* 41, no. 2 (January 23, 2013): 102, https://doi.org/10.1080/19325037.2010.10599134.

18   Amschler and McKenzie, "Perceived Sleepiness," 102.

Do you struggle with getting to bed at a decent time or falling asleep once your head hits the pillow? Here are a few tips for getting to sleep and staying asleep:

× Don't work right up until you go to sleep.
× Limit screen time in the hour before going to sleep.
× Go to sleep at the same time every night.
× Exercise during the day.
× Avoid caffeine in the afternoon and evening.
× Get blackout curtains.
× Wear a mouthguard if you grind your teeth.
× Wear an eye mask.
× Wear earplugs.
× Use separate bedding from your partner if they tend to wake you up. If you've ever been to Europe, you know this is the norm there. Make up a double or larger bed with two twin top sheets and coverlets. Your partner's tossing and turning is a lot less likely to wake you up!
× Create a nighttime routine to get your mind and body ready to sleep.

## KEY TAKEAWAYS

1. Keep up with your medical appointments by scheduling them ahead of time.
2. Use your sick days.
3. Make grooming and clothing choices that make you feel good.
4. Find a form of exercise that feels good and is sustainable.
5. Prioritize sleep.
6. Cut down on sugar and drink water.
7. Meal prep to help you make healthy choices.

# Reflection

Take some time to reflect on your physical self-care and answer these questions:

 × How are you currently practicing physical self-care? What are you doing well in this area?
 × In what ways are you struggling with physical self-care?

Pick one area of physical self-care where you can begin to make improvement immediately. Create a concrete goal for yourself, which includes how and when you will implement this activity or goal.

*Here are a few examples:*

 × *Starting tonight, I will set a daily alarm for 10:00 p.m. and begin getting ready for bed at that time. I will go to bed by 10:30 p.m.*
 × *This afternoon I will purchase a reusable water bottle. Every morning I will fill the water bottle before school and finish the bottle before I leave school.*
 × *Every quarter I will use at least one of my paid days off.*
 × *Tomorrow I will purchase ingredients for healthy smoothies. At least three out of five days a week, I will make and drink a smoothie instead of skipping breakfast.*
 × *This weekend I will look for a dentist. By the end of next week, I will schedule my first appointment.*
 × *On Tuesdays and Thursdays every week, I will change into running clothes as soon as I get home and run one mile.*

Whatever your goal is, make sure you are specific! If your goal is simply to eat better, you may not know where to start. Instead, create a habit to help you achieve this goal, such as the plan for breakfast smoothies above.

## EMOTIONAL SELF-CARE

Emotional and mental health does not mean being happy all the time. Being emotionally healthy means that you can experience and manage your emotions. The teacher world (especially on social media!) is filled with platitudes about staying positive and "choosing happy." Of course, it's good to be positive—and I hope you're happy most of the time—but ultimately, experiencing a range of emotions is part of being human. If you're upset about a situation, trying to force yourself to be happy about it generally doesn't fix the situation. Often, our feelings indicate that something is wrong and needs to be addressed. There's nothing inherently wrong with feeling frustrated, stressed, angry, overwhelmed, or any other "negative" emotion. Acknowledge and accept your emotions and then consider what you can do to manage or improve them.

Your emotions are affected by just about every other form of well-being discussed in this book, and it's impossible to isolate them. If you find yourself anxious, cranky, or sad without a clear reason, try going through this checklist of basic needs and make sure they're being met:

* Have you eaten in the last few hours?
* Have you had enough water today?
* Did you get enough sleep last night?
* Have you showered in the last twenty-four hours?
* Have you had time for yourself recently?
* Have you exercised within the last few days?
* Have you taken your medications?

Often, when you make sure those basic needs are met, your mood improves. You can think of your emotions as a warning signal to make sure you meet these needs. Don't ignore them or beat yourself up for having emotions. Acknowledge them and be thankful for them.

## Mental Health

But what if taking care of your basic needs doesn't improve your mood? What if your emotions start to feel out of control and you find yourself anxious or sad most of the time?

Nearly one in five adults in the United States has a mental illness.[19] So if you're reading this book, there's a good chance you may live with a mental illness, the most common of which is anxiety.

I discovered I have Generalized Anxiety Disorder in high school and Panic Attack Disorder in college. I began taking medication near the end of college and began regular talk therapy in my final year of teaching. When I've talked about my anxiety disorder publicly, many, many teachers have reached out to me to share that they are dealing with the same thing.

I'm not a mental health professional, so instead of telling you how to treat your mental illness I'm going to tell you to PLEASE seek help from a mental health professional. Medication and therapy have both changed my life and allowed me to have the happy, relatively stable life I have today. Don't deny yourself that opportunity.

## Therapy

Whether you have a diagnosed mental illness or not, I strongly urge you to try therapy if you're struggling in any way. People tend to think therapy is cost-prohibitive, and in some cases, it is. But as teachers, most of us are lucky enough to have insurance and the cost is often only a small co-pay ($25/session in my case), or a certain number of sessions may be completely covered. Not sure what your insurance will cover? Call the

---

19   Substance Abuse and Mental Health Services Administration, *Key Substance Use and Mental Health Indicators in the United States: Results from the 2018 National Survey on Drug Use and Health* (HHS Publication No. PEP19-5068, NSDUH Series H-54) (Rockville, MD: Center for Behavioral Health Statistics and Quality, Substance Abuse and Mental Health Services Administration), 2019, retrieved from https://www.samhsa.gov/data/, 43.

number on the back of your card and just ask! I've done this for myself and others, and it's pretty simple.

Therapy is such an important part of my life now that I sometimes forget it holds a stigma until I see how hesitant some people are to go. I've talked to many people who feel they aren't doing badly enough to go to therapy. That's not how it works! Therapy shouldn't be a last resort or a source of shame. I went weekly for years and now go every other week. I've gone to marriage therapy. If I have children, I will no doubt go to family therapy. I've encouraged just about every member of my family to go to therapy.

Wondering what to talk about in a therapy session? Here are some ideas:

* Feelings about your job
* Relationships with coworkers
* Worries and fears
* Next steps in your life
* Relationship with a partner
* Relationships with friends and family
* Stressors

Therapy can truly be a game changer. And I promise that just about any therapist is used to seeing teachers! If you're stressed out and overwhelmed, a therapist can be just the outside perspective you need. Family and friends are great, but they may not always feel it's their place to intervene, or if they do, you might not take them seriously. And coworkers, of course, are likely to be dealing with the very same stressors. If your first therapist isn't a good fit, don't give up and assume therapy just isn't for you. It's okay to try a few different therapists.

You don't need a diagnosis of a mental illness to go to therapy. It's perfectly okay to go just for help dealing with a specific situation, such as with your job, partner, or family.

If you're even just thinking about it, please—go to therapy!

## Affirmations

In many ways, the most important part of self-care is the mindset shift of prioritizing your own well-being. Platitudes like "students first" and "in it for the outcome, not the income," may be well-intentioned, but I prefer this quote: "What's good for teachers is good for students." For many, the idea that we are deserving of as much care and love as our students is a radical one. If we are used to the feeling that doing what's best for kids or being successful means collapsing exhausted and uncared for into bed at night, then practicing self-care can be a significant shift, and not always an easy or comfortable one. My therapist once reminded me: "You're allowed to do something just because you enjoy it." Insert mind-blown emoji here. This was not a mindset I had as I worked four jobs at a time through college, or as a first-year teacher also attending grad school, or even just as a regular old teacher. For me, affirmations were a critical part of successfully making the self-care mindset shift.

Start by reading through the following affirmations, out loud if you can. Mark the ones that resonate with you. If one makes you feel emotional, it is likely something you need to internalize.

*I am peaceful and calm, and greet the day with ease.*
*I believe in myself and my abilities.*
*I am making a difference in the world.*
*I am thankful to be a teacher.*
*I treat myself and my students with kindness.*
*I deserve to be happy.*
*Taking care of myself is important and necessary.*

*I choose to set healthy boundaries.*
*I am a priority in my own life.*
*I am patient with myself.*
*I am competent and capable.*
*My time outside school is my own.*
*I treat myself with compassion.*
*I am learning to take better care of myself.*
*I take care of myself first.*
*I love, accept, and appreciate myself.*
*I am enough, I have enough, I do enough.*
*I give myself permission to do what is right for me.*
*I give myself the care and attention I deserve.*
*Self-care is not selfish.*
*I am a person of high integrity and sincere purpose.*[20]
*I have earned my rest for tonight.*

There are many ways to use affirmations, so find the way that's right for you. Here are some ideas:

* Write them in a journal or on a sheet of paper and read them aloud at a certain time each day.
* Record them as a voice memo on your phone, saying each affirmation twice. Play the recording on your way to work or at another time, reciting the repetition of each affirmation along with the recording.
* Write them on sticky notes and post them on your mirror. Say them aloud as you're getting ready for work.
* Type or write each affirmation on a notecard and place the cards on a ring. Flip through the cards and read each affirmation aloud.
* Write an affirmation in large letters on a piece of paper and tape it where you'll see it right when you wake up.

20   Edmund J. Bourne, *The Anxiety & Phobia Workbook*, 4th ed., (Oakland, CA: New Harbinger Publications, Inc., 2005), 295.

Whichever method you choose, be sure to develop a routine and say your affirmations every day. Affirmations are most effective when recited regularly. I chose the voice memo method, and sometimes listened to and recited my affirmations multiple times on the way to work. I found it to have a big effect on my mindset. You can also recall these affirmations throughout the day as you need them, and you'll remember them more readily if you've already recited them that day. Post-mental breakdown, you could often find me muttering, "I am patient and calm, and greet the day with ease," as I marched up or down stairwells from class to class. I also found "I am a person of high integrity and sincere purpose" helpful as I navigated relationships with co-teachers and began setting boundaries.

Affirmations become the way we speak to ourselves. And speaking to ourselves in a calm, supportive way instead of berating ourselves is so powerful. It can be uncomfortable to say affirmations aloud at first, and I completely understand if it feels a bit silly or cheesy. Try to have a sense of humor about it! If I'm feeling guilty about spending time on a puzzle, I might shout at my husband, "It's okay to do things just because I enjoy them! Self-care is not selfish!" As a college student, I lived briefly with my older sister and had an affirmation on the wall that read, "You are brave." She rearranged the letters to say, "U R a boy raver," and still regularly says this to me whenever we come across a mantra or inspirational quote. It's okay that it feels funny to make positive statements to or about yourself. That doesn't mean they're not effective. I urge you to give it a try for a few weeks, even if you're not sure how you feel about it.

Affirmations can also be a great way to help you get to sleep. You may find your mind racing as you lie in bed, worrying about students or tasks left undone. I found "I am enough, I have enough, I do enough" to be a great affirmation to calm my mind at night. "I have earned my rest for tonight" is great for reminding yourself that you deserve rest.

You can also find lots of affirmations specific to your needs by searching online. One of my favorite resources, *The Anxiety & Phobia Workbook* by Edmund J. Bourne, has several pages of affirmations specifically for people with anxiety.

## Journaling

Journaling is a great form of self-care in and of itself, but it can also help you monitor your progress on your self-care journey. Keeping a journal is inexpensive, requires minimal tools, and doesn't have to take much time. You can have a dedicated journal, or it can be a file on your computer, a note in your phone, or a section of your planner. I use a bullet journal for just about everything in my life, so I keep my journal in a separate section there. Personally, I prefer to write using pen and paper, as being on my computer or phone tends to feel like work for me—and also feels less confidential. But do whatever is easiest and most comfortable for you!

I think many of us have experienced simply feeling better after getting our thoughts down on paper, but it turns out there are many well-documented benefits of journaling. They include:

- ✕ Reduced stress
- ✕ Decreased feelings of depression[21]
- ✕ Increased working memory[22]
- ✕ Reduced intrusive thoughts[23]
- ✕ Increased immune functioning[24]

---

21  Katherine M. Krpan, et al., "An Everyday Activity as a Treatment for Depression: The Benefits of Expressive Writing for People Diagnosed with Major Depressive Disorder," *Journal of Affective Disorders* 150, no. 3 (September 25, 2013), https://doi.org/10.1016/j.jad.2013.05.065.

22  Kitty Klein and Adriel Boals, "Expressive Writing Can Increase Working Memory Capacity," *Journal of Experimental Psychology: General* 130, no. 3 (2001): 520, https://doi.org/10.1037/0096-3445.130.3.520.

23  Klein and Boals, "Expressive Writing Can Increase Working Memory Capacity," 520.

24  Bridget Murray, "Writing to Heal," *Monitor on Psychology* 33, no. 6 (June 2002), https://www.apa.org/monitor/jun02/writing.

Not sure what to write? Try these journaling prompts:

* How am I doing?
* What is going well in my life?
* Why is it going well? (Consider your own actions and others', fortunate circumstances, etc.)
* What am I thankful for?
* What am I looking forward to?
* How am I taking care of myself?
* What am I struggling with?
* How am I feeling?
* What can I do to take better care of myself?

## Mindfulness & Meditation

While I am putting mindfulness and meditation under emotional self-care, it could easily go under both physical and spiritual self-care. Being mindful and practicing meditation have a myriad of benefits, but since the most immediate impact is likely on your mood, I chose to place it in the emotional self-care section.

The benefits of mindfulness have been widely researched. Here are just a few, as reported in *Monitor on Psychology*[25]:

* Lessened stress, anxiety, and depression
* Increased life satisfaction
* Improved cognitive performance
* Increased focus and concentration
* Increased tolerance and patience
* Lower blood pressure
* Fewer physical health problems

My primary experience with both mindfulness and meditation has been through kundalini yoga. If you missed it in the exercise section, kundalini yoga is a meditation-based form

25  Daphne M. Davis and Jeffrey A. Hayes, "What Are the Benefits of Mindfulness," *Monitor on Psychology* 43, no. 7 (July/August 2012), https://www.apa.org/monitor/2012/07-08/ce-corner.

of yoga that still incorporates exercise. If you are looking to become more mindful, regularly practicing kundalini yoga is a wonderful way to do so. You have to be quiet to hear yourself think. I know that I personally tend to live life at such a frantic pace that I never truly have time to process. Often I go into yoga with something weighing on my mind, and while I wasn't consciously thinking about it during class, I come out with an answer. In fact, that's how I decided to self-publish this book rather than accept the contract I had been offered. We often know what's best for us, or what we really want, deep down. But if we don't give ourselves the opportunity to slow down, it's hard to access that clarity.

You don't have to attend a class to practice mindfulness, though I find it to be helpful in remaining consistent. You can be mindful while driving to school, preparing your meals, or going on a walk. Mindfulness is awareness. And we so often drown out this awareness by checking our phones, letting the TV play in the background, or worrying about events in the past or future. Because our days as teachers are often so frantic and full, we have to be very intentional about cultivating mindfulness.

Here are a few of my favorite things to do mindfully:

× Make granola. I measure each ingredient carefully, and notice the texture and smell as I chop them and add them to a mixing bowl. This makes it a routine I enjoy, rather than a chore.

× Prepare a bath. Before taking a bath, I fill the water and pour in bath salts or a bath bomb. I put on a bathrobe. I light candles.

× Go for a walk. I'm lucky enough to live next to Lake Michigan. With or without my dogs, I walk along the lakeshore path without music or a podcast, observing the water and trees, noticing each step I take.

* ✕ Fold laundry. Ever since switching to the folding method prescribed in *The Life-Changing Magic of Tidying Up*, I've enjoyed neatly folding my clothes and putting them where they belong.

Take a moment to think about your own life and where you might be able to practice mindfulness in your day-to-day activities. What are you already doing on a regular basis that may lend itself to this practice? What might you want to add to your life to allow you an opportunity for practicing mindfulness?

My friend Becca Wertheim, a current school administrator, 2017–18 Asheville Teacher of the Year, and creator of the e-course *Teach with Peace*, is one of the most mindful people I know, so I asked her to share her perspective on mindfulness and self-care. Here's what she had to say:

*As a beginning teacher, I thought that being the best teacher I could be meant pouring all my energy into my classroom. My self-care was compromised and I found myself feeling more stressed than fulfilled. I was falling out of love with teaching. I knew I had to make a shift. I realized that if I wanted to give my students the best version of myself then I needed to dig deeply to become the best version of myself. Mindfulness helped me do that. Slowing down, connecting with my body, and using positive affirmations helped turn my stress into awareness and my awareness into a new relationship with teaching. I started listening more carefully to my body and learned how to use my breathing to ease nerves, anxiety, and discomfort. Mindfulness also helped me set healthy boundaries in my life so that I could protect and preserve my energy. Mindfulness taught me that although there are a lot of things in education that are out of my control, what I can control is my breathing, my awareness, and my intentions. I bring it to students through the use of affirmations, intention-setting, gratitude practice, morning mindfulness circles, mindful moments throughout the day, and yoga brain breaks. Mindfulness shows us the power of the mind-body connection and is such an important tool for teachers and students. You can learn more in Teach with Peace, my 7-day mindfulness course for educators.*

If you want to learn more about mindfulness for teachers, Becca's course is a great resource, and so is the book *Happy Teachers Change the World* by Thich Nhat Hanh and Katherine Weare. It's a wonderful guide for cultivating mindfulness specifically for teachers. The preface of the book states, "By embodying mindfulness, concentration, joy, and peace, educators can bring happiness, stability, and clarity to their community,"[26] which I find to be such a beautiful and true statement.

### Gratitude

Almost anything you read on the topic of happiness or self-care will likely mention gratitude.

Like practicing mindfulness (and the two are often intertwined), feeling gratitude has many documented benefits that go beyond what you might expect. Here are a few Robert Emmons outlines in his book *Thanks!*[27]:

- × Increased life satisfaction
- × Easier time falling asleep and better-quality sleep
- × Increased optimism
- × Stronger connections with others
- × Increased well-being of spouse

---

26   Thich Nhat Hanh and Katherine Weare, *Happy Teachers Change the World: A Guide for Cultivating Mindfulness in Education* (Berkeley, California: Parallax Press, 2017), xxxi.

27   Robert A. Emmons, *Thanks!: How the New Science of Gratitude Can Make You Happier.* (New York: Houghton Mifflin Harcourt, 2007), 11, 33–34.

- Stronger relationship with partner
- May help prevent depression
- Decreased feelings of loneliness

While you can't magically become a more grateful person overnight, you can absolutely cultivate gratitude in your life. The more consistent you are, the more likely you are to see positive and long-lasting effects. So whichever method or methods you choose, be sure to incorporate them into your life so that you'll actually practice them. Like most other practices, an accountability partner can help you stay consistent. Maybe you and your partner can commit to completing one of these activities together during or after dinner each night. Try incorporating one into your morning meeting with your students—kids are the best at reminding you when you've forgotten to do something! Here are some ideas for cultivating gratitude to get you started:

- Think of three things you're thankful for each night as you fall asleep.
- Keep a gratitude journal and record what you're thankful for each day. This is one of the best researched forms of cultivating gratitude. It's most effective when you write in a journal every day and when you elaborate a bit on what you're grateful for, rather than just listing them.[28] This is also a great routine to get into with your students.
- Create a gratitude jar. Cut up strips of paper and place them near a mason jar or another container. Fill out one strip a day with something you're grateful for and place it in the jar. Take out a few strips and read them when you need a reminder of the good things in your life.
- Try texting or sending a message of gratitude to a different person in your life every day for a week. The message can

---

28  Emmons, *Thanks!*, 190.

be as simple as, "Thanks for being a great co-teacher," or "Thank you for always being there for me."

* Write a thank-you note. Once a week, or even once a month, write a letter or email to someone in your life you're thankful for. It will make both you and the recipient feel great.

* Replace comparison with gratitude. When you start to feel jealous of someone else's life, accept and acknowledge the feeling, but then also let the feeling be a trigger to remind you to be thankful for the good things in your own life. For example, if you find yourself thinking, "I wish I only had twenty kids in my class like Ms. So-and-so next door," accept the feeling, but then also express gratitude for the positive things about your own class.

* Give a gift of thanks. Don't do this if it will add stress to your life, but if you enjoy giving or making gifts, give one to someone you're thankful for, just because. Bring a coffee for your co-teacher, send a family member flowers, or gift a friend or student a book you love. It will give both of you that warm, fuzzy feeling!

* Appreciate your partner. Partners of teachers may find themselves doing more than the average significant other. Whether it's packing your lunch, accepting that you fall asleep at 9 p.m. every Friday night, or helping you set up your classroom, take the time to express your gratitude to them for being there for you.

* Say thank you to your students. When I was in Teach for America training, I was always told not to thank my students because it will make them feel like what I tell them is optional, not mandatory. That, teacher-friend, is bullshit. Saying thank you and expressing gratitude toward your students will go a long way in establishing rapport and building a warm classroom community. Research has

shown that being thanked motivates people to engage in more helpful acts.[29] So thanking your students will benefit your own well-being, and will hopefully encourage your students to continue to be helpful as well!

× Recite a gratitude affirmation each day. One of my dogs has a chronic illness, and I am truly grateful for each day I have with him. To remind myself of this when I don't quite feel like getting out of bed in the morning, I say to myself, "I am thankful for another day to spend with Hippo." Yours might be, "I'm thankful for another day to make a difference in students' lives," or even just, "I am grateful to be alive." This little reminder can boost your mood and start your day off in a positive way.

× Create visual reminders. I can vividly recall the weathered red sign we had in my childhood home that read, "count your blessings." I can't say it actually encouraged me to count my blessings, mostly because I came to hate the phrase because my mother frequently used it as a response to any complaint I had. However, visual reminders can be effective, especially if you keep them fresh. For me, something that looks out of place, like a sticky note on my mirror, is more likely to catch my attention than some tasteful decor nestled on a shelf.

## Self-Compassion & Self-Love

In Becca Wertheim's e-course *Teach with Peace*, she asks participants to treat ourselves as we would a student. How would we treat a student if they were down, disappointed in themselves, or anxious? We wouldn't berate them the way we sometimes do ourselves. We would comfort them and treat them gently. I teared up a little bit during that exercise. I had never extended

---

29   Francis J. Flynn, "Frank Flynn: "Gratitude, the Gift That Keeps on Giving," Stanford Graduate School of Business, March 1, 2012, https://www.gsb.stanford.edu/insights/frank-flynn-gratitude-gift-keeps-giving.

the compassion I had for my students to myself. "We need to acknowledge that what is good for others is good for ourselves," Skovholt and Trotter-Mathison write in their book, *The Resilient Practitioner*.[30] If we want so badly to care for others, if we want others to be happy, are we, too, not worthy of caring and happiness?

My yoga teacher ended our class the other night with a quote from Yogi Bhajan: "Happiness is your birthright. Live it." If you need to reckon with this idea, reckon with it. Write, attend therapy, talk about it with your partner. Because this, I believe, is at the heart of the mindset shift needed to truly take care of oneself. You must start with the recognition that you—yes you!—are worthy of caring and happiness. Self-love is the heart of self-care.

Learning to love yourself and treat yourself kindly can be a difficult journey, but it's a necessary one. If we can't love and accept ourselves, it's difficult to truly love and accept others, including our students.

What are some ways you can begin to feel self-love and practice self-compassion? Here are just a few ideas:

- Practice positive self-talk, including affirmations.
- Celebrate your achievements.
- Forgive yourself for your mistakes.
- Give yourself a compliment. You can even fill a journal page with all the things you like about yourself.
- Accept compliments from others.
- Recognize your feelings, even when they're negative.
- Engage in activities you enjoy, just because you enjoy them.
- Find a therapist you click with and attend therapy regularly.
- Read anything by Brené Brown.

---

30  Thomas M. Skovholt and Michelle Trotter-Mathison, *The Resilient Practitioner: Burnout and Compassion Fatigue Prevention and Self-Care Strategies for the Helping Professions*, 3rd ed. (New York: Routledge, 2016), 163.

## Social Media

When I began teaching in 2013, I didn't know "teachergram," or really any online teaching community, existed at all. When I first started finding teacher blogs and Instagram accounts, I was thrilled! Having had little to no training, it was great to find blog posts outlining how to do things like set up a sight word center, or even just tips for getting posters to stay up on cinderblock walls. Still, as I became more involved in the teacher Instagram world, I got frustrated. I saw things like "gift trees" filled with tags with items parents could buy for the classroom, while I quite literally had to buy my own copy paper. On teacher appreciation day, I'd see other teachers receive small mountains of gifts, while my coworkers and I were lucky if our administration put some candy in the teachers' lounge. While overall I'm still thankful for the internet, and don't quite know how teachers ever taught without it, it did contribute to a feeling of bitterness about my own school and situation.

Some teachers (perhaps you!) have been inundated with images of Pinterest-perfect classrooms since they were student teachers. I've received more and more messages from young teachers who feel pressured to have color-coordinated classrooms, create elaborate anchor charts, and "transform" their classroom every two weeks. There's nothing wrong with those things, IF you have your actual teaching, classroom management, and self-care under control. While I love learning and sharing on social media, I can't help but think that some accounts create an unrealistic expectation of what teaching is really like, or should be like.

Interestingly, the research so far shows that social media is neither good nor bad for your mental health, as a whole. In one study, positive interactions on social media correlated to decreased depression and anxiety, and negative interactions correlated to higher levels of depression and anxiety.[31] Consider whether your interactions on social media are mostly negative or positive. Positive interactions include chatting with friends and family, liking and enjoying others' photos and posts, and sharing about your own life. Negative interactions include comparing yourself to others, "hate following" accounts, and consistently criticizing others. Start noticing how you feel after scrolling through Instagram or checking Facebook. Do you feel inspired and refreshed? Or do you feel stressed out and annoyed?

If you find social media negatively impacting your well-being, it's time to start practicing better social media self-care. Here are a few ideas:

* **Limit your time on social media.** It's SO tempting to check Instagram or Facebook whenever you have a spare second. Use those spare minutes to take a few deep breaths or stretch instead. Set specific times you'll check social media throughout the day—maybe it's for five minutes as you eat your breakfast and then another fifteen minutes after school. Monitor how it makes you feel and adjust accordingly.

* **Conduct a social media cleanse.** Which accounts do you really connect with? Which ones inspire you? Keep those and delete the rest. You can always go back and hit follow again later if you find yourself missing someone in your feed.

* **Take a social media break.** If social media's getting you down, take a break altogether! Make it one day, one week, or one month—whatever you need and feel you can stick to! Observe how you feel without it.

---

31   Elizabeth M. Seabrook, Margaret L. Kern, and Nikki S. Rickard, "Social Networking Sites, Depression, and Anxiety: A Systematic Review," *JMIR Mental Health* 3, no. 4 (2016): e50, https://doi.org/10.2196/mental.5842.

* Remove social media apps from your phone. If you want to check social media less often, make it a bit more difficult for yourself by removing the apps from your phone. You can still access them through a browser when you really want to.
* Stop checking social media before bed. The last thing you want to do before you try to sleep is to give your mind more things to race about!

## KEY TAKEAWAYS

1. Feeling a variety of emotions is healthy and normal.
2. If you are struggling with your mental health, seek professional help.
3. Affirmations and journaling are both ways you can improve your mental health.
4. Incorporating mindfulness and gratitude into your life has many different positive benefits.
5. If social media is negatively affecting you, limit your time on it and/or conduct a social media cleanse.

## Reflection

Take some time to reflect on your emotional self-care and answer these questions:

× How are you currently practicing emotional self-care? What are you doing well in this area?

× In what ways are you struggling with emotional self-care?

Pick one area of emotional self-care that you can begin to make improvement in immediately. Create a concrete goal for yourself, which includes how and when you will implement this activity or goal.

*Here are a few examples:*

× This weekend I will research possible therapists. By the end of next week, I will schedule my first therapy appointment.

× Tonight I will write an affirmation on a sticky note and put it on my bathroom mirror. Each morning, starting tomorrow, I will say the affirmation aloud to myself as I get ready for work.

× Tomorrow I will find or buy a notebook or journal. I will place it on my bedside table, and each night I will write one thing I am thankful for before I go to sleep.

× Starting tonight, I will not check my social media accounts after 9 p.m.

## SPIRITUAL SELF-CARE

I'm not religious, so spiritual self-care is not something I've always prioritized. If you are religious, you likely already know the benefits. Whether you are religious or not, connecting with your spiritual side and feeling a sense of peace and wholeness is important for your well-being. While the exact effects of a spiritual practice are hard to measure, studies of religious and spiritual interventions found that these interventions decreased stress, alcoholism, and depression.[32] Many studies found an overall increase of well-being associated with religious and spiritual interventions. That said, there are also reports of increased feelings of guilt, abandonment, and punishment associated with religion[33], so it's important that you find the practice that's right for you.

As a kid, I didn't understand why my deeply religious mother said that going to mass in the morning made her whole day better. Now, as an adult, it makes sense. When I meditate or say affirmations in the morning, it changes my mindset and helps me have a more peaceful day.

To gather insight from a religious perspective, I reached out to my friend Asmahan Mashrah, a teacher, mom, and practicing Muslim. Here's what she had to say:

*Growing up I wasn't really interested in faith; it wasn't until my mid-twenties when I started to feel that I was missing something and felt incomplete. I was also extremely over-whelmed, as a single mother, transitioning and navigating being married again, finishing my master's and working full time I felt like I was being pulled into a million directions.*

32   J. P. B. Gonçalves, G. Lucchetti, P. R. Menezes, and H. Vallada, "Religious and Spiritual Interventions in Mental Health Care: A Systematic Review and Meta-Analysis of Randomized Controlled Clinical Trials," *Psychological Medicine* 45, no. 14 (October 2015): 2937, https://doi.org/10.1017/S0033291715001166.

33   Gonçalves, Lucchetti, Menezes, and Vallada, "Religious and Spiritual Interventions in Mental Health Care," 2938.

*As a Muslim we are obligated to pray five times a day, our prayers last five minutes, and I found space during those times to reconnect with myself. That is also when I started to be intentional in my prayer; I started to listen to podcasts and lectures in English, have discussions with people about certain topics, and indulge in research. I began to feel my stress and worries melt away. My relationship to Allah (GOD) gave me purpose and peace. Being able to have that time to pray, make supplication, ask GOD for better, and disconnect from the world for a few minutes was a way I took care of myself and rejuvenated my spirit to be able to provide for my family and give the proper energy to my life. Self-care through faith saved me. Self-care is vital for your physical and mental health, whether it be through meditation, a few minutes a day to yourself or praying for your wishes, putting yourself first will allow you to be better for everybody else.*

*You can learn more from Asmahan on Instagram @asmahanmashrah.*

Not sure where to start? Here are a few ways to practice spiritual self-care:
- ✘ Attend a religious service for your faith.
- ✘ Meditate.
- ✘ Practice a meditative form of yoga, such as kundalini yoga.
- ✘ Spend time in nature.
- ✘ Journal.
- ✘ Pray.
- ✘ Read a spiritual book.
- ✘ Listen to peaceful music.
- ✘ Practice mindfulness.
- ✘ Have quiet time.
- ✘ Express gratitude.

× Connect with those who have similar spiritual beliefs.

× Practice deep, focused breathing.

× Create an altar or shrine with objects that are meaningful to you.

× Perform a ritual. (You can find ideas for rituals in the next section.)

## Rituals

Those of us who were raised in an organized religion may associate rituals only with religion, and most religions do, in fact, include plenty of rituals, from saying grace before meals to bat mitzvahs. However, rituals can be a way of practicing spiritual self-care, even if you're not religious or don't believe in a god. Rituals can be a form of comfort, celebration, and connection. Here a few rituals to try:

× Plant a seed or repot a store-bought plant while setting an intention. You can even record the intention and place it nearby. Remember your intention when you care for your new plant.

× Go stargazing.

× Attend a gong or sound bath. My kundalini yoga studio hosts these occasionally—try searching for gong bath or sound meditation and the name of the nearest city to find one near you.

× Take an extra-special bath. Try lighting candles, placing crystals nearby, and using a special bath bomb or bath salts.

× Create a vision board at the beginning of a new school year, calendar year, or season.

× Take time each month to set five intentions and record them in your journal.

× Create a morning mindfulness ritual. Each morning, I try to take fifteen to twenty minutes to sit down and journal, read mindfulness books, and meditate before I do anything else.

## KEY TAKEAWAYS

1. You don't need to be religious to practice spiritual self-care.
2. Conducting rituals is a great way to nourish your spiritual side.

## Reflection

Take some time to reflect on your spiritual self-care and answer these questions:

× How are you currently practicing spiritual self-care? What are you doing well in this area? Remember that your way of connecting with your spirituality may not be traditionally religious, though of course it can be!

× In what ways are you struggling with spiritual self-care?

Pick one area of spiritual self-care where you can begin to make improvement immediately. Create a concrete goal for yourself, which includes how and when you will implement this activity or goal.

*Here are a few examples:*

× This weekend I will go to the bookstore or library and pick out a spiritual book that resonates with me. I will read it at least three nights a week before I go to sleep.

× Starting tomorrow, I will meditate or pray for three minutes each morning as my coffee brews.

× One day a week I will attend a faith-based meeting at my place of worship.

## SOCIAL SELF-CARE

Humans need community. As an introvert, I've sometimes felt that the best way to practice self-care is to just be alone. If you're introverted like me, spending all day with people can be draining, and it's true that you do need alone time to recharge. But, ultimately, social isolation negatively impacts your well-being. Hopefully, you already have a strong community full of supportive family, friends, and coworkers. If you don't, or aren't feeling connected, try some of these ways to practice social self-care:

× Call a close friend or family member who doesn't live nearby. You can even set up a weekly or monthly phone date if you have trouble remembering to call.

× Have a weekly or biweekly happy hour. The social worker from my first school (who became a close friend, and was even the officiant at my wedding!) and I had a happy hour every other Friday after school.

× Join a club or team that meets regularly.

× Go to a trivia night with a friend.

× Volunteer at your local animal shelter or another organization.

× Start a family text thread. My two older sisters and I have a text thread we communicate through daily that helps us keep in touch, even though I live in a different state.

× Have a weekly roommate dinner.

× Attend a class and make an effort to get to know the other students.

One thing you might notice about most of these suggestions is that they're scheduled. Like many forms of self-care, social self-care can be hard to prioritize if you don't plan it ahead of time. A standing phone date, club meeting, or happy hour gives you something to look forward to, and it also gives you time to plan accordingly.

## Friendships with Coworkers

Being friendly with and getting along with your coworkers will, of course, make your time at school more pleasant. But a word of caution: make sure your whole social life doesn't revolve around your school. As teachers, we spend enough time at school and thinking about school. If your social self-care only consists of hanging out with coworkers and talking about (or complaining about!) school, it's not much of a form of self-care at all.

Some groups of teachers have a negative energy, and if this is the case at your school, you may be better off being friendly, but not too involved. For instance, in one of the schools I taught at, there was an intense amount of drama within a group of teachers that had all taught there for about the same amount of time. They began as friends, but in the high-stress environment of our school, tensions would rise *so* quickly, and it became uncomfortable to try to navigate. Allegiances were constantly shifting, people entered and left giant text threads, and friendships ended over who was or wasn't invited to what outing. There were days I dreaded going into a teacher's classroom because I didn't know where she and I stood based on the ongoing drama of this group. In retrospect, I wish I had handled these social dynamics differently. As a new teacher at the school, I was eager to be accepted and appreciated that this group included me. Looking back, I should have made more of an effort to get to know *all* my coworkers, not just the members of this particular group. Some gossip is perhaps inevitable, but I could have done more to curb it and keep myself neutral. While there is nothing wrong with socializing with your coworkers, I think I would have been happier and less stressed if I had focused more on my social life outside of school, or at least diversified my friendships within the workplace.

I wouldn't want you to isolate yourself, but at the end of the day (or the school year!), it's better to be on cordial terms with everyone than not know who's your best friend and who's your mortal enemy.

I was always impressed by how one of my fellow special education teachers at my last school, Tony Romeo, navigated social interactions with our coworkers. Like me, he worked with many different teachers across grade levels when providing inclusion services. Unlike me, he seemed to be on good terms with just about everyone in the school and managed to be welcomed in all the various social circles without being involved in pettiness or drama. We've remained friends, so I reached out to Tony to get his thoughts on how he stays on good terms with his coworkers. Here's what he had to say:

*In every work environment we have positive and negative influences on our individual goals. In the field of education, everyone begins their career with the goal of helping children learn. How we all work toward that goal changes with our unique perspectives and individual experiences—and our own opinions—but our initial reason for working with students is to help them learn. Teachers and educational staff may push and pull against which path to take toward their interpretation of how to help children learn. It often feels uncomfortable to see a coworker make a choice which diverges from our own. Taking the time to consider why they made that totally different decision can help to grow your understanding or, frankly, just make you feel more frustrated. If empathizing with another educational professional isn't helping, accept your frustration and give yourself a break for not understanding whatever that person just did. Then, remember that they probably deserve a break too; we are all (in theory) working toward the same goal. If you feel more conflict with the situation, vent to other educational peers, let your frustration out, and maybe try to think of how you may have handled the situation differently. Would your idea have worked? Remember, none of us have all the answers.*

Approaching your coworkers with empathy and grace can go a long way toward making your social life at school more peaceful.

## KEY TAKEAWAYS

1. Schedule in social time with friends and family.
2. Be sure to have a social life outside of school and coworkers.

## Reflection

Take some time to reflect on your social self-care and answer these questions:

× How are you currently practicing social self-care? What are you doing well in this area?

× In what ways are you struggling with social self-care?

Pick one area of social self-care where you can begin to make improvement immediately. Create a concrete goal for yourself, which includes how and when you will implement this activity or goal.

*Here are a few examples:*

× Tonight I will reach out to a long-distance friend and schedule a phone date for next week.

× This weekend I will research local clubs and groups that match my interests. I will attend a meeting for one by the end of this month.

× Starting tomorrow, I will excuse myself from work conversations that are exclusively gossip.

## INTELLECTUAL SELF-CARE

I don't see intellectual self-care brought up very often in the teaching world, perhaps because teachers tend to love learning and don't need many reminders to keep their brains active. Intellectual self-care is just that—keeping your brain healthy by exercising it. Practicing intellectual self-care can also keep you from feeling bored or stuck. Just because you're teaching six-year-olds doesn't mean your intellectual interests can't go beyond skip counting and sight words.

Many of us are so wrapped up in teaching that we may not seek out much intellectual stimulation beyond the education world. I know there are many great education podcasts out there, but you might want to limit how many you listen to if they stress you out. It's great to stay up-to-date on the latest education research, but it's also healthy to have outside interests. Take a minute to think of a few topics you're interested in. Mine include true crime, archaeology, travel, and design. Need ideas? Read through the list below and circle at least three that interest you.

| | | |
|---|---|---|
| politics | sports | environmentalism |
| science | business | fashion |
| religion | health | food |
| design | philosophy | crafts |
| archaeology | social justice | world cultures |
| history | feminism | astronomy |
| true crime | current events | animals |
| math | pop culture | architecture |
| music | technology | photography |
| folklore | arts | literature |

Keep your chosen topics in mind when seeking out forms of intellectual self-care. Here are some examples of ways you might practice intellectual self-care:

* Learn a new language. Apps like Duolingo make it easy to practice.
* Visit a museum.
* Go to the library.
* Read a nonfiction book on a topic you're interested in.
* Read the newspaper.
* Listen to an educational podcast.
* Watch a documentary.
* Learn a new skill.
* Take a class.
* Listen to NPR.
* Attend a lecture.
* Write an essay or story.
* Read a longform article. Longform.org has a ton of great ones archived!
* Complete a crossword puzzle or other brain puzzle.
* Join a club centered on one of your topics of interest.
* Write a letter to the editor.
* Read a niche magazine.

**KEY TAKEAWAYS**

1. Self-care includes seeking out intellectual stimulation beyond teaching.
2. You can practice self-care by engaging with your interests through reading, listening, writing, watching, learning, etc.

## *Reflection*

Take some time to reflect on your current intellectual self-care and answer these questions:

× How are you currently practicing intellectual self-care? What are you doing well in this area?

× In what ways are you struggling with intellectual self-care?

Pick one area of intellectual self-care where you can begin to make improvement immediately. Create a concrete goal for yourself, which includes how and when you will implement this activity or goal.

*Here are a few examples:*

× Once a month I will go to the library and pick out a nonfiction book to read.

× Next weekend I will visit a museum I've been wanting to check out.

× This weekend I will listen to an education podcast as I do laundry.

## VOCATIONAL SELF-CARE

Vocational self-care is having a fulfilling job that is a good fit for you. Not every position will be a good fit for you. Not every school will be either.

We discussed burnout earlier, and one of the primary aims of helping teachers practice self-care is to prevent burnout. However, much of the research around burnout shows that the work environment, rather than the individual, is the highest risk factor. Maslach and Leiter outline the factors that affect work environment and risk of burnout in "Early Predictors of Job Burnout and Engagement" as workload, control, reward, community, fairness, and values.[34] Let's take a closer look at each of these factors.

**Workload:** Maslach and Leiter define work overload as when the "job demands exceeding human limits."[35] That sounds . . . familiar. This poses the highest risk for burnout when there's no recovery period. Perhaps you find yourself tasked with an unreasonable amount of work when IEP season comes around, or at the end of each grading period. If you have time to recover between these stressful events, you're not necessarily going to burn out. The real problem is when these crises never cease. If you feel like you are constantly being asked to take on another task with an urgent deadline . . . and another one . . . and then another one, you may be facing work overload.

**Control:** When you have more control over your work, you're less likely to burn out. For example, even though it required more work on my end initially, I appreciated being able to make my own schedule as a special education teacher. When an administrator decided she would make the special education schedules one year, I found it endlessly frustrating. I was

---

34    Christina Maslach and Michael P. Leiter, "Early Predictors of Job Burnout and Engagement," *Journal of Applied Psychology* 93, no. 3 (May 2008): 500.

35    Maslach and Leiter, "Early Predictors of Job Burnout and Engagement," 500.

forced to follow a schedule that I knew made me less effective. This schedule included me "pushing in" for inclusion minutes for twenty minutes at a time and split-up groups of students I knew were on the same level and worked well together. This directly contributed to feelings of negativity and cynicism—a key component of burnout. I'm sure you have examples of this in your own setting, whether it's being forced to use a scripted curriculum or being told you have to level your library, even when you know it's not best practice.

**Reward:** A lack of sufficient reward, including financially and socially, for doing your job well can lead to burnout. I don't need to tell you that teachers are underpaid. In many cases, this is out of your school's control. Social rewards, on the other hand, *are* within your school and administration's control. Social rewards are basically acts of appreciation. Genuine praise and recognition can go a long way for teachers, just as with students.

Each year, Chicago Public Schools issues schools a score based on a ton of different factors. My friend's school recently received their updated score: it remained a 2, the second lowest score a school can receive. The low, unchanged score in and of itself already represents a lack of reward, but then her administration compounded the effect by holding a staff meeting and scolding the teachers for their role in the low score. I was enraged to hear this. I can just imagine those teachers walking out of that meeting thinking, "Why do I even try? Our score never goes up and we just get yelled at no matter how hard we work." The administration could have helped mitigate the negative effect of the low score by praising the effort the staff had been making and laying out a plan of how they planned to raise the score next year with staff help. It's easy to see how incidents like this can contribute to teacher burnout.

**Community:** Positive social interactions at work lower the risk of burnout. It's not hard to see why: if you don't like anyone at work, and no one likes you, you're not going to feel positively about your job. Inclusive staff breakfasts, happy hours, and holiday parties can help foster a sense of community.

**Fairness:** In an attempt to ration the copy paper my school knew would run out long before the school year ended, the administration allotted each teacher a certain number of reams a month. Oh, except special education teachers, who weren't allotted any because, apparently, we don't use paper. The unfairness of this situation was one of many that hardened me against my administration, as inconsequential as it may seem. I'm sure many of us have told our students or our own children that life isn't fair. It's true that a certain amount of unfairness is to be expected and can be tolerated, but when you face inequity in your job day after day, it will likely lead to negativity and cynicism.

**Values:** If your values don't align with those of your workplace, it can actually increase all three components of burnout: exhaustion, cynicism, and inefficacy.[36] Many of us are willing to work extremely hard if we believe we are all working together toward the same common goal. When we begin to think that our co-teacher doesn't actually care whether kids learn to read, or that our administration only cares about test scores, there is a conflict of values.

## When It's Time for Change

This book is largely about what *you* can do to practice better self-care and create a sustainable career as a teacher. So why did I include the work environment risk factors for burnout? Because I don't want anyone to think that if you just buck up and start journaling and going to the gym more the teacher burnout problem will be solved. Part of vocational self-care is

---

36    Maslach and Leiter, "Early Predictors of Job Burnout and Engagement," 501.

making sure you're in an environment that won't lead you to burnout.

As a teacher, was I personally doing things that increased my risk for burnout? Yes. Additionally, I score strongly on the personality quality that puts you at the highest risk of burnout—neuroticism. But even if those things weren't true, I would have still been at a high risk for burnout because my school was on the negative end of the spectrum for all the work environment factors above.

Take a hard look at your own school. If your school has a high workload, but you feel appreciated and have a strong community there, you may be able to avoid burnout by setting firm boundaries. If your social interactions at school aren't the best, but the rest of the factors are manageable, you can likely avoid burnout by helping cultivate a better community at school yourself, and by being sure to practice social self-care outside of school. But if you read through those factors and thought to yourself that your school was on the negative end of the spectrum for every one? It's probably time for a change.

This next part is tricky. I don't take telling anyone to leave their school or teaching altogether lightly. Teaching is an incredibly important job. We need all the good teachers we can get. But at some schools, it's hard to feel like it's even possible to succeed. After my mental breakdown in my final year of teaching, I began to take a step back and realize that, perhaps, not everything was my fault or even under my control. What I was being asked to do was not reasonable. It felt like it was *not possible* to do a good job. Having learned more about burnout since then, I realize I was going through a period of detachment. I was beginning to distance myself from the demands of teaching.

Having taught at a charter school for two years, and then at a traditional public school for another two, I didn't want to just continue hopping from school to school. I began to suspect that all schools were terrible and that the only way out was . . . out. Again, now I see that was the burnout talking. So if you're feeling that same way, let me state for the record: Not all schools are terrible. Not all administrators are tyrants. Not every teacher is on the verge of collapse.

It's okay to make a change though. You do not have to stay at a school where you are treated badly. If there's a specific issue that needs fixing, it's worth trying to solve it, but you don't need to languish in a school where you can't thrive for the rest of your life.

What if your school seems okay on all or most of these *and* you're practicing strong self-care, but you're still not happy with your job? It's possible teaching full time just isn't a good fit for you, and that's okay. You don't have to stay a classroom teacher. There are other ways to help kids. You can be an education consultant, you can be a teaching coach, you can be a special education case manager. You can leave education altogether. I don't say this because I want you to leave or think it's the only path forward. But you shouldn't feel trapped. You have options.

### Self-Care at School

Even if you love your school and position, the school day can still get stressful! Let's talk about some specific ways you can integrate self-care into your school day, since you likely spend at least half of your waking hours there.

×   **Involve your students.** One of the best ways to practice self-care at school is to do so with your students. Try incorporating mindfulness that you can practice along with your students into your day. Gonoodle.com, a site for brain breaks, has several good mindfulness and yoga videos you can play for a quick refresh for both you and your students.

× **Take a breath.** Deep breaths are free and you can take one any time! If I feel overwhelmed with a situation or student, it helps so much to take a deep breath before responding. This is also great modeling for students!

× **Avoid negative venting or gossip.** Some amount of complaining or venting among coworkers is natural, and in my opinion, inevitable. However, constantly talking about and focusing on the negative is called rumination, and it's bad for your mental health. Excessive rumination is linked to both anxiety and depression. Try changing the topic, or limit your time with consistently negative coworkers.

× **Plan your prep periods.** Planning what you'll do during your prep period will keep you focused and free up time on your nights and weekends. You might even try a prep schedule. For example, Monday is for grading, Tuesday is for lesson planning, Wednesday is for making copies, etc.

× **Wear comfortable clothes you feel good in.** Try planning your outfits for the week on Sunday so that you always have something you like ready to wear.

× **Bring a healthy snack.** Avoid sugary snacks in the teachers' lounge during prep periods by bringing your own healthy snack or treat, like fruit, popcorn, or dark chocolate.

× **Create an environment you enjoy spending time in.** This doesn't have to drain your bank account! Organizing and eliminating clutter is one of the best ways to create a peaceful environment, and it's free! Try using a single color for your bulletin boards and simple borders to create a more soothing space. Plants are a great natural way to make your classroom or office feel more pleasant. I highly recommend *The Life-Changing Magic of Tidying Up* by Marie Kondo if you need help changing your mindset about hanging on to objects. You can also refer to the Environmental Self-Care section of this book for more ideas (pages 106-109).

× **Establish solutions for common stressful situations.** Take a minute to write down some of your most frequent stressors at school. For me, I frequently lost my key or got locked out of my classroom. There's a very simple solution—wear a lanyard! And yet, it took me years to implement. Broken copy machines are another common point of frustration. Can you make your copies further ahead of time so a broken machine won't derail all your plans? Can you make fewer copies by projecting questions on the board and having students record their answers on blank paper? Is a specific teacher always late picking up her students from your class? Sit down and have an honest conversation with that teacher, and come up with a backup plan just in case the conversation isn't effective.

× **Diffuse tension.** As an introvert and someone with social anxiety, tense situations between coworkers were a HUGE source of stress for me and honestly made me not want to go to work some days. Communication can solve or at least de-escalate a lot of these situations. Rather than ignoring or retaliating snubs or gossip, try sitting down with the coworker in question and being honest. It's awkward and uncomfortable, but clearing the air now will lead to a healthier environment for everyone.

× **Keep a self-care kit at school.** Here are some ideas of what to include: lip balm, hair tie, cough drops, essential oils, lotion, affirmation cards, dark chocolate, a packet of tea. Read more on this in the Special Activities for Self-Care section (pages 113–116).

× **Say no.** No one is going to intervene for you and insist that no, you can't take on that extra IEP, or no, you're not going to sub all day in another class with no notice. Your school, your principal, your coworkers—they're not going to stop you from burning yourself out and becoming bitter and tired. I had to learn that I am responsible for my own well-being, and I had to learn to take that responsibility seriously. Rightly or wrongly, people probably aren't going to stop demanding things from you any time soon. It's okay to say no. No one else is going to say it for you.

## Set Boundaries

Setting boundaries is both critical and extremely difficult for many teachers. Many can easily get behind the idea of "treat yourself!" and get a pedicure once in a while. What's much harder is setting firm boundaries and sticking with them.

As a first-year teacher through Teach for America, I was told it was best practice to make parent phone calls every night. Standing on a crowded bus on the way home from a three-hour grad school class at 9:30 p.m., most nights I heard at least one of my fellow first-year teachers making parent calls through their headphones. On the bus. After a full day of teaching and then three hours of grad school. At 9:30 p.m. I have no doubt they had amazing parent relationships. Maybe they even made "transformational change" ("transformational" is TFA's favorite word) in their classroom. But not many of my TFA friends are teaching anymore (a common and valid criticism of TFA). And if they are, they've had to work through those unreasonable expectations we were fed and learn how to set healthy boundaries.

While only a small percentage of teachers go through TFA, the lack of boundaries and unhealthy expectations go way beyond that organization. We are told that we, and we alone, are responsible for a student's success. With that burden, we work early mornings, late nights, and through our lunches and sick days. It's not fair and it's not effective. The martyr-teacher WILL leave. Or, if they don't, they become bitter and disillusioned.

So let's set some boundaries. Fill in the blanks and check the boxes that you can commit to.

- ☐ I will leave school by _____.
- ☐ I will do, at most, _____ (length of time) of work at home.
- ☐ I will not spend more than _____ (length of time) working on the weekend.
- ☐ I will not check my email after _____.
- ☐ I will not keep my school email on my phone.
- ☐ I will not check my email on the weekend.
- ☐ I will not take parent phone calls after _____.
- ☐ I will not be on more than _____ committee(s).

You likely have your own unique boundaries to add. For special education teachers, perhaps it's: I will not spend more than three hours on an IEP. For teachers with large classes, perhaps it's: I will only grade two assignments per student per week.

Setting these boundaries is the first step. Sticking to them is the next and harder step. Saying no is hard, teacher-friends. Most of us are helpers, and often achievers by nature. Our principal asks us to head up a committee and we feel obligated to say yes. There's a stack of papers to grade on our desk and we feel pressured to stay late and grade them. We need to be ready for these pressures.

In his book *Atomic Habits*, James Clear explains the power of making your habits a part of your identity. Saying to yourself or others, "I leave school by 4:00 every day," or better yet, "I am the kind of teacher who leaves by 4:00 every day because I value my well-being and work efficiently during the day" is more effective than, "I try not to stay too late at school."[37] Be clear with your boundaries and add accountability measures. While I was teaching (post-mental breakdown), I committed to not working after 8:30 p.m. on Sunday nights, and to taking a bath at that time. I told my husband this, I told my therapist this, and, for the most part, I stuck with it. Committing to that boundary and act of self-care is more effective than saying, "I will try to take better care of myself," or "I will try to do something nice for myself one day a week."

Harder to share boundaries with than a spouse or therapist—who of course care about you and WANT you to take better care of yourself—are coworkers and principals. As a special education co-teacher, I was very aware that any work I didn't do might shift to my co-teacher. As a general education teacher, you might feel this with your grade level team. There was another special education teacher at my school who told her co-teachers she wouldn't be doing any work after contract hours or on weekends. She also let them know she wouldn't be modifying any work if they didn't let her know at least two days in advance. I admired her chutzpah, but I won't lie and tell you that this went over well with anyone.

I think there's a middle ground here, one that can keep our coworkers and supervisors reasonably happy with us, without sacrificing our own well-being. Let your coworkers know the reasons for your boundaries and what you're going through, to the extent you're comfortable. I had a great working relationship with my last co-teacher, and she knew I had an anxiety disorder and was going to therapy. When I told her I would be using a few of my sick days for my own mental health, she was supportive of that. It made life harder for her, because subs are scarce and often aren't super helpful in an inclusion setting. But

---

37 James Clear, *Atomic Habits: An Easy & Proven Way to Build Good Habits & Break Bad Ones* (New York: Penguin Random House, 2018), 34.

she knew I cared about the students, and that I was just trying to care about myself too. Schools can, unfortunately, become catty environments. It's easy to feel resentful when we're all overworked and underpaid.

So, how we can all encourage each other to practice better self-care, rather than seeing it as a zero-sum game? Try approaching it more collaboratively. Instead of saying you won't be modifying assignments without a two-day notice, perhaps you could meet with your co-teacher and let her know that last-minute modifying is really difficult for you and makes it challenging to fully meet the students' needs. "Could we meet weekly instead and lay out the assignments for the week so I know what's coming up and can plan accordingly?" If you're going to take more of your sick days this year (which I encourage!), perhaps you can say, "I think it's really important, as teachers, that we take care of ourselves and use our benefits, so I'm going to be taking my sick days this year. Is this something you want to try to do too? Maybe we can help each other with sub plans so those days still go as smoothly as possible."

You may not be your principal's favorite teacher, what with your sick-day-taking and leaving-on-time. Some people wrongly consider staying late to be an indication of a good teacher. But there is no prize for having the last car in the staff parking lot. Hopefully your principal is aware of the importance of teacher wellness and will respect your boundaries. I almost cried when a principal emailed me to let me know she was ordering three Teacher Care Crates (my self-care subscription box for teachers) to distribute among her staff each month. Awareness is growing, but again—especially in under-resourced schools, where the principal him or herself is likely to be under a lot of pressure—teacher well-being may be the last thing on your principal's mind.

Accept that you may not be the principal's pet (which hey, can result in extra work anyway!), but know that with clear communication you can still be a valued teacher. If you get a chance to meet with your principal or supervisor, the conversation might go something like this, "I wanted to let you know that I am really trying to have a better work-life balance this year so I can have a sustainable career as a teacher. I won't be checking my email after 7:00 p.m. or on Saturdays. You might see me leaving school earlier, but I'll be working hard during the day to use my time efficiently."

Even the most thoughtful conversations may still result in some bitterness. But hopefully, you will also lead by example and can be part of creating a healthier culture for teachers at your school. Better a few muttered words when you leave school at 4:00 than a mental breakdown that results in you leaving the profession.

## Self-Care & the Side Hustle

It's no secret that many teachers have second jobs. If you've taught in a school recently, it's also not a secret that many of these jobs involve selling something. You won't hear me knocking the side hustle—after all, my side hustle is now my full-time job. But carefully consider whether the money you make is worth the time and energy you spend doing the work.

Over the course of a school year, I might be asked to buy essential oils, nutritional shakes, jewelry, clothing, and makeup through various multi-level marketing businesses other teachers participate in. Many of us feel obligated to buy something when invited to these in-person or online "parties." Let's say that out of thirty teachers, we're all selling something, and each of the other twenty-nine teachers buys something from the other teachers for $20. Each teacher spends $580 over the course of the year, but, assuming they're making about

20 percent commission on each item they sell, they're only making $116. These kinds of business models are basically just passing money around, except everyone's losing 80 percent of the money they spend. Many also suggest you'll only do minimal work for potentially a lot of money. The truth is, many participants in multi-level marketing spend hours and hours each week trying to promote their business and don't ever make enough money to be worth the hours put in—some even go into debt.

I've included this information because I don't want you to waste your precious personal time on an endeavor that may never earn you any money, and will likely cause additional stress. If you're considering participating in a multi-level marketing program (or are already involved in one), be sure to carefully consider all aspects of the program and whether the work will be worth the reward—or if there even will be a reward. If you're involved in a program that requires a lot of time and yields little profit, there's no shame in "quitting" your side hustle so you can make better use of your time elsewhere. If you need a second job to make ends meet, consider something that is fun for you in some way and won't result in a heavy workload or stress outside of your working hours.

Looking for something that's flexible and can be done from home? Try one of these options:

- × Teach English online to children overseas. There are several popular companies that pay a decent hourly rate for teaching English to Chinese children, and they prepare all the lessons for you.
- × Sell your educational resources online. There is NO guarantee that you will become a big seller, but if you feel you have some unique resources and like to create, try uploading a few products to Teachers Pay Teachers or a similar site and see how they do.

- × Take up pet sitting. If you love animals, sites like Rover. com make it easy to start pet sitting. If you're uncomfortable with pet sitting during your busy week, you can do just weekends and holidays, which are some of the most popular times for pet sitting anyway.
- × Become a virtual assistant (VA). Many online-based business owners hire VAs to help with tasks. As a teacher, you're uniquely well-suited to being a VA for educational resource sellers. Personally, I pay my sister to work remotely and proofread my resources and complete a few other tasks. Ask around!

Whatever you do, make sure it's worth the income you're generating. As a teacher in Chicago Public Schools, I personally found that my teacher salary was enough for me as a single adult. However, I know that's not the case in many districts, especially if you have children. If your pay is so low you don't ever see being able to quit your second job, you might want to consider moving to another district or pursuing a degree or certification that will raise your salary. Teaching is difficult enough without the added pressure of a second job.

## KEY TAKEAWAYS

1. Your school environment may be putting you at a high risk of burnout. Consider if it's sustainable for you to stay at your current school long-term.

2. You can incorporate acts of self-care throughout your day at school.

3. Setting firm boundaries is critical to practicing vocational self-care.

4. If you are working a second job or have a side hustle, carefully consider whether it is worth the time and effort you are putting in.

## *Reflection*

Take some time to reflect on your vocational self-care and answer these questions:

× How are you currently practicing vocational self-care? What are you doing well in this area?

× In what ways are you struggling with vocational self-care?

Pick one area of vocational self-care where you can begin to make improvement immediately. Create a concrete goal for yourself, which includes how and when you will implement this activity or goal.

*Here are a few examples:*

× *This weekend I will create a weekly prep period schedule. I will keep it in my planner or posted at my teacher desk and follow it to make the best use of my preps.*

× *Starting next week, I will leave school by 4:00 at least four out of five days a week.*

× *Starting tomorrow, I will incorporate a mindful brain break for students and myself between our reading and math times.*

## ENVIRONMENTAL SELF-CARE

Environmental self-care refers to spending time in healthy environments. This can be a particularly challenging area of self-care for teachers. We spend most of our time at school and at home. We have a limited amount of control over our school environment, and many of us feel we don't have the time or energy to make our home environments as comfortable as we'd like.

Let's start with your home. Your apartment or house should be a place where you can relax. This doesn't have to mean an expensively decorated home straight out of a design magazine; it should just be a clean and cozy place that makes you feel comfortable. Here are some ways you can make that happen:

- **Declutter.** And keep only what you really love or need. The easiest way to keep your stuff from taking over your home is to have less of it.
- **Make a cleaning schedule.** It can be hard to keep up with the tasks that keep our homes clean and comfortable. Make a weekly or monthly schedule of cleaning tasks so you don't become overwhelmed, and make sure you divide the tasks equitably with anyone else living in your space.
- **Maintain a comfortable temperature.** For years, I've lived in apartments without air conditioning units and with poor heating. Being too hot or too cold can make it impossible to relax. Invest in a window air conditioning unit, a space heater, a fan, an electric blanket . . . whatever you need to do! You can find many of these items affordably on Facebook Marketplace or Craigslist.
- **Incorporate plants around your home.** Nature has a calming effect and can even increase concentration and memory retention. If you've never had a plant before or are worried you won't be able to care for it, go to your

local garden center and ask for help choosing a plant that is low-maintenance.

× **Make a list.** Feeling overwhelmed by a messy or unpleasant home? Try coming up with a list of tasks and doing one each weekend. For example, organize your kitchen one weekend and wash your couch cushions another. If you have a large list of tasks that will be difficult for you to do yourself, hire a handyman for the afternoon, if you can afford it. We did this recently after moving into an older home, and it was such a relief to have all our doorknobs working and pictures hung in one afternoon.

× **Take advantage of summer.** If you're able to take the summer off, or even just work fewer hours, this can be a great time to tackle some home projects that will make your living environment better for the following school year.

× **Create a special self-care space in your home.** See the Special Activities for Self-Care section (pages 113–116) for more details.

Now, let's move on to your classroom. You may not be able to control much of the environment at your school, but you do have some control over the space where you spend most your time. Here are some ideas for making your classroom a more pleasant and healthy environment, not only for you, but for your students:

× **Streamline your classroom colors and/or decor.** If your classroom decor makes you feel even a little bit overwhelmed, chances are it could be causing some sensory issues for your students too. Try picking one or two colors and sticking with them for most classroom items. If you have lots of items hanging from the ceiling, consider taking them down or putting them all in one area so that most of the ceiling is clear.

× **Get rid of stuff.** There is so much STUFF that goes along with having twenty-plus kids in your classroom all day. Backpacks, jackets, pencils, textbooks, worksheets, laptops . . . the list goes on. Most of it is nonnegotiable, so focus on eliminating the things you DON'T need. Do you have thirty textbooks stacked up that you don't use? You probably shouldn't throw them out, but see if you can move them to a storage area or basement. Many of us inherit another teacher's stuff when we move into a new classroom. If you're not using it, see if another teacher in your school wants it. If not, donate, recycle, or toss it.

× **Adjust the lighting.** If your classroom has harsh lighting, consider dimming the lights with magnetic light covers or keeping your shades open for natural light.

× **Consider getting a classroom plant.** A plant has the same benefits in your classroom as it does in your house, plus students love watering plants and watching them grow.

× **Designate space for others.** If you have other teachers or clinicians working in your room, designate a spot for their materials. One of my general education coworkers did this for me, and it kept my papers and tools from spreading all over the classroom.

## KEY TAKEAWAYS

1. Decluttering will make both your home and classroom more pleasant places.
2. Plants and natural light are great ways to improve any space.

## *Reflection*

Take some time to reflect on your environmental self-care and answer these questions:

× How are you currently practicing environmental self-care? What are you doing well in this area?

× In what ways are you struggling with environmental self-care?

Pick one area of environmental self-care where you can begin to make improvement immediately. Create a concrete goal for yourself, which includes how and when you will implement this activity or goal.

*Here are a few examples:*

× This weekend I will make a cleaning schedule for myself and my roommates/partner.

× Tomorrow I will visit a nursery and pick up one plant for my apartment and one for my classroom.

× When I next change up my bulletin boards, I will use the same color for all of them and leave one blank.

## Part 3:

# ESTABLISHING YOUR SELF-CARE PRACTICE

**W**hat does self-care look like for you? After reading this far, you may already have a clear vision of how you're going to take care of yourself to ensure you're bringing the best version of you to the classroom each day. Perhaps you're still not sure what exactly self-care means for you—that's okay! The most important thing is to embrace the idea that self-care is essential, not selfish—and then look for the ways you can best fulfill your sacred obligation to take care of yourself. In this section, we'll explore how to make self-care work for *you*.

## YOUR SELF-CARE DOESN'T HAVE TO LOOK LIKE EVERYONE ELSE'S SELF-CARE

The classic self-care for women seems to be "get your nails done." For me, getting a manicure isn't really self-care. Interacting with strangers piques my social anxiety, I feel awkward while the nail technician paints my nails, and I'm incapable of not smudging them afterward. I'll go with a friend if they want to, or before a big event, but it's not something I'm going to choose to spend money or time on. I'd much rather spend the $24 for a day pass to the local Korean spa. No one speaks to you (unless you get a scrub and the woman will say "face up," "face down," and that's about it), and it's a blissful few hours with my phone turned off and tucked away in my locker. The idea of going to a mostly nude spa by yourself and getting scrubbed within an inch of your life doesn't seem to appeal to most people, and that's fine.

Think about what activities you truly enjoy. What nourishes you? What makes you feel refreshed and reenergized afterward? If you haven't been practicing self-care up until now, it may take some time to figure that out. Try the activities in this book, but don't feel pressured to keep up with one if it's not something that nourishes you. Think about what you liked to do as a child. Did you like to read? Do puzzles? Play outside? Draw? Play board games? Try out some of these activities again and see how they make you feel. I asked teachers on social media what some of their more unusual forms of self-care are, and I thought I'd share a few of the responses to give you some ideas!

- Folding laundry
- Listening to funny podcasts
- Organizing things
- Waking up early to watch the sunrise
- Running errands alone
- Completing crosswords
- People watching

## MONEY WELL-SPENT

I realize that many teachers reading this are likely struggling to make ends meet. However, if you have some financial cushion or can rearrange your budget accordingly, here are some purchases and services that I think could help many teachers practice better self-care:

- **Buying classroom resources online.** For some reason, as a teacher, I felt like $15 was an exorbitant price to pay for a whole downloadable unit when I'd have no problem dropping $30 on a sweater at Target on a whim. Not everything on sites like Teachers Pay Teachers is high-quality. But if you come across a resource that can save you hours and hours of time? Buy it. Your school should be providing you with the resources you need, and it's unfair to spend your own money on classroom resources. But I would rather you spend $15 than lose fifteen hours of your precious time.

× **Trying meal kits.** As discussed in the nutrition section, meal kits can be a great way to make sure you're eating healthy without having to meal plan or grocery shop.

× **Investing in cleaning services.** If you can afford to have someone else clean your home, even if it's only every few months, this can make your home more pleasant and free up some of your own time.

## SPECIAL ACTIVITIES FOR SELF-CARE

Hopefully at this point you have lots of ideas for how to practice better self-care. But if you're overwhelmed or looking for more specifics, I've put together some special activities for self-care you can do right now!

### Start a Self-Care Journal

Purchase a special journal or decorate one you already have with stickers or a collage. Use it to record your self-care calendar and your favorite affirmations. Create a habit-tracking section to track the self-care routines you're trying to incorporate. You can even create a section for each area of self-care as outlined in this book: physical, emotional, spiritual, social, intellectual, vocational, and environmental. Write about what aspects of each area you're doing well with, and what aspects could use improvement. Use the rest as a journal. When you're struggling, come back to your self-care journal to remind yourself of how and why to practice self-care.

## Create a Collage

Collaging is a great way to express yourself and get in touch with your inner child. Gather old magazines or print some images you like off the internet. Start cutting and gluing! Need some ideas? Try making a collage of things that make you happy, or make a vision board of what you want for your life. If you're not feeling crafty, you can create a digital version using a Pinterest board (you can make it secret if you like!) or even just in a PowerPoint file.

When I first started going to therapy, I created a collage of what makes me happy to remind myself of what I was giving up by working all the time. I posted it above my desk at home as a reminder to make sure I made time for what makes me happy.

## Plan a Self-Care Day

Dedicate a mental health day or weekend day to self-care! This can include practical self-care, like a doctor's appointment or haircut, but make sure it includes plenty of activities you truly enjoy too. Most importantly, no schoolwork! Try creating an actual schedule of your day so that work doesn't sneak in. Of course, you can splurge with a spa day, but don't feel like a self-care day has to be expensive! Here's an example of how I might schedule out a day of self-care:

| | |
|---|---|
| **9:30** | Wake up and make coffee |
| **10:00** | Work on puzzle in my pajamas while listening to an audiobook and drinking coffee |
| **11:00** | Take my time getting ready and wear a favorite outfit |
| **12:00** | Make myself a nice lunch or eat at a local cafe |

**1:00**  Work on a personal project, like knitting a sweater
**2:00**  Take my dogs on a long walk or head to a local nature area
**4:00**  Go to a needed appointment, like therapy, a haircut, or a doctor's appointment
**5:30**  Attend an evening yoga class
**7:00**  Enjoy cooking a healthy dinner and eat with my spouse
**8:30**  Take a luxurious bath
**9:30**  Read before bed

I know many teachers might read this, especially those with kids, and think there's no way they have time for this. It might seem frivolous, but you NEED time to nurture yourself in order to keep up with the demands of teaching, as well as those in the rest of your life. If you can't bring yourself to carve out a whole self-care day, try a self-care morning, afternoon, or evening. If you have kids and a partner, communicate to them how important this is for you and your well-being. If you don't have a partner, perhaps you can trade childcare with another teacher so you can both have time for at least a self-care half-day.

**Create a Self-Care Kit for School**
No, a drawer full of candy does not count as a self-care kit! Dedicate a pouch, drawer, or box at school for items to help you practice self-care. Here are a few ideas of what to include:
* Calming tea
* Hair ties and/or bobby pins
* Lip balm
* A calming essential oil roller
* A healthy snack
* Affirmation cards—you can purchase these or write your own on index cards

- ✘ Lotion
- ✘ Deodorant
- ✘ A photo of someone or something you love

When you're having a hard time, your kit will be there waiting for you. You can take a few minutes during your prep to make a cup of tea, apply some lip balm or lotion, and read your affirmations. It may not fix whatever problem you're facing, but hopefully it will help you approach it in a calmer way.

### Create a Sacred Self-Care Area Just for You in Your Home

Many of us have a cool-down corner in our classrooms for students, so what about creating an adult version for yourself? It can be in a guest bedroom, a home office, or just a corner of your bedroom! It could include a comfy armchair or just a floor pillow or yoga mat. Put some items to help you practice self-care in a basket, like your journal, a coloring book, and an eye pillow. If you can, try to use this area *just* for self-care. That way, when you go there, your mind and body will be ready to relax. Use this space for yoga, journaling, meditating, or just relaxing. In my home, we have a small library-type room adjacent to the living room full of shelves. I set up a chair and table in the corner and keep my basket of self-care items on a shelf. This is where I practice my morning mindfulness routine. I know I might not always have this area as our family grows and changes, but I will be sure to incorporate a self-care space somewhere else when it does.

## CREATE A SELF-CARE PLAN

Throughout this book, I've asked you to reflect on your current self-care and identify self-care goals. Now it's time to put everything you've learned together to create a self-care plan. Feel free to make a copy of this page or draw your own chart in a notebook or on a piece of paper. As you're filling in your own plan, be sure to include the goals you created at the end of the self-care category. You can highlight these goals or put a star by them to indicate that they're a priority.

| | Every day I will... | Every week I will... | Every month I will... | Other Intervals |
|---|---|---|---|---|
| Physical Self-Care | | | | |
| Emotional Self-Care | | | | |
| Spiritual Self-Care | | | | |
| Social Self-Care | | | | |
| Intellectual Self-Care | | | | |
| Vocational Self-Care | | | | |
| Environmental Self-Care | | | | |

I've included my own self-care plan to give you some ideas. All of this reflects my actual self-care plan, except the vocational section, which I modified to reflect what it might look like if I were currently in the classroom.

| | Every day I will... | Every week I will... | Every month I will... | Other Intervals |
|---|---|---|---|---|
| Physical Self-Care | -Eat three meals a day -Drink at least one water bottle full of water -Walk my dogs -Sleep 8 hours a night -Take medications | -Go to yoga -Meal prep lunches for the week -Take a bath | | -Every 6 months, I will see the dentist -Every year, I will see my primary care doctor, allergist, and ophthalmologist -I will stay home when I have a fever or am throwing up |
| Emotional Self-Care | -Take my anxiety medication -Say my affirmations | -Go to therapy -Write in my journal | | -Every 6 months, I will see my psychiatrist |
| Spiritual Self-Care | -Have quiet time in the morning | -Go to yoga | | |
| Social Self-Care | -Text or talk with a friend or family member | -Do something fun with a friend | -Host or attend a party or other gathering | |
| Intellectual Self-Care | -Read something that interests me | | -Visit somewhere new that interests me, like a museum or exhibit | |

| | Every day I will... | Every week I will... | Every month I will... | Other Intervals |
|---|---|---|---|---|
| **Vocational Self-Care** | -Leave school by 4 pm <br> -Not check my school email after 7 pm <br> -Be productive during my prep <br> -Avoid gossip | -Spend one weekend day not working at all <br> -Limit my weekly lesson planning to 3 hours | | -Every quarter I will take a mental health day <br> -Every year I will reevaluate whether I want to stay in my current position and school |
| **Environmental Self-Care** | -Make my bed | -Vacuum the house <br> -Wash sheets | -Schedule a cleaning service | |

Don't worry about filling in every single square, as not all the intervals will make sense for your specific self-care habits. Feel free to flip back to each self-care section to find some ideas!

After creating your self-care plan, display it somewhere you'll see regularly. You can post it on your refrigerator or tape it in your teacher planner. The more visible you make it, the more likely you are to remember to follow your plan! You can even make checking in with your plan part of your plan! Undoubtedly, you won't follow your plan 100 percent of the time. But you don't need to make your self-care plan one more thing to beat yourself up about. Check in with your plan regularly to make sure it's realistic and doable for you. For example, if you've specified that you want to go on a run every day, but you currently *never* run, you might want to adjust your plan to running one to two times a week. If you've scheduled in weekly meal prep, but never have the time to do it, consider how you need to adjust. Maybe you can offload this task to your partner or maybe "meal prep" needs to consist of buying healthy frozen meals for the time being. Don't let perfect be the enemy of good!

## DEALING WITH ADDITIONAL RESPONSIBILITIES

Teaching alone is enough to make self-care difficult to prioritize, but every teacher has more going on in life than "just" teaching. Other factors, from being a parent to dealing with a chronic illness, can have a serious impact on how well you are able to take care of yourself. While I hope that you can apply the previous sections of this book to your life regardless of your specific circumstances, we'll dive into some common additional responsibilities many teachers face in this chapter.

### Parenting

Though I'm currently pregnant with my first child as I write this book, I did not experience teaching as a parent. As a teacher, I was in awe of my colleagues who managed to balance the needs of their students as well as their own children. I did not see how I could possibly have children myself and maintain the amount of time and energy I put into my job. And, in fact, I couldn't have. It turns out, I couldn't maintain it even *without* children.

While there is no question that having your own children makes your job as a teacher more challenging, I have also made some interesting observations from my conversations with teacher-parents. As a teacher without children or other significant outside responsibilities, it is possible to pour your entire being into teaching. Your job is teaching, your hobbies are teaching, your friends are teachers. This isn't healthy, and it's not sustainable. For teacher-parents, on the other hand, this isn't possible. It's just not. For most parents, you just can't stay at school until 7 p.m., whether papers need grading or not. You can't go into school every weekend, because you have your own kids to care for, soccer games to attend, and memories to make. For many parents, I think it becomes easier to set boundaries, because your family comes before your job. For teachers without children, that distinction is not always there. Unfortunately, while you may find it easier to separate yourself from teaching as your only identity as a parent, it also decreases your already limited time to practice self-care.

Since I haven't had the experience of teaching as a parent myself, I reached out to my friend LaNesha Tabb. LaNesha is an incredible teacher who also creates resources for teachers and regularly presents at national conferences. She also has a husband and two young children and (at least from what I see on social media!) seems to balance all these things beautifully! Here's what she had to say about self-care as a teacher-parent:

*I (like you probably are) am busy. I just am. I teach full time and manage a business on the side. I am also a wife and mother of two. People ask me all of the time, "How do you do it all? How do you manage to teach, hop a plane for a conference, put out a new t-shirt line, release a new resource, and bake keto-goodies with your kids?" Well, friends, I want to share two things.*

*1) I don't. I don't "do it all" and I don't want to. I do things sometimes and tend to share those things on social media. So, the old adage stands—don't assume anything about anyone's life on social media! It truly is a highlight reel—as much I hate to admit that.*

*2) Behind this "busy" (and often overwhelmed) teacher-mom is a husband that is quite literally a superhero. I don't know how he does it. He cleans. He organizes. He pays the bills, plays with the kids, and anything else you can think of. I say this from the most humble position possible because it wasn't always like that . . . and that was my fault.*

*Let's chat just a minute about "roles." I spent the first few years of our marriage attempting to be all of the things that I thought a woman was supposed to be. I tried to teach full time, run my business (which was much smaller at the time, but, still), and attempt to be June Cleaver on top of all that. My husband would offer to help but I refused because "that's my job." I had attached my value in our relationship to this. Finally, I had to learn that I just couldn't do it all. We had a conversation about our gifts and realized that not only was my husband good at organizing, planning, and household tasks—he actually enjoyed it! We decided that for our family, operating within our gifts would eventually be for the benefit of us and our children. It was hard at first because our society has brainwashed us into thinking that we must operate within antiquated gender roles. So, in the name of self-care, I had to reevaluate my expectations for myself. I had to redefine what our normal would look like. It wasn't easy, but I was able to love myself enough to let some of these expectations go and in doing so, I was able to better care for myself and my family. And for me, that's real self-care.*

*You can find LaNesha at educationwithanapron.com and on Instagram @apron_education.*

Many teacher-parents I've talked to, particularly mothers, have echoed what LaNesha discovered about partners and gender roles. In heterosexual partnerships with children, women today are still more likely to do the majority of housework and childcare, regardless of whether they work full time, or even whether they are the primary earner. This is unfair, regardless of your profession, but as a teacher, it's outrageous. Your partner simply must take on an equal or greater share of household duties, depending on their own profession. If your partner is unwilling, then some things will have to go undone, or, if possible, you can outsource tasks like cleaning or laundry. If you're a single parent, you have to be even more ruthless about your school boundaries, as well as willing to simply let things go. Perhaps you can have it all, in the sense that you can be both a great teacher and a loving parent, but unquestionably you cannot *do* it all.

As a teacher, you likely already feel the constant pressure of work you could be doing, from perfecting lesson plans to prepping centers. As a parent, I imagine that list of tasks doubles, to include everything from folding laundry to researching summer camps. Just like a teacher without children, you have to take care of yourself first. Your own self-care practice is just as essential as the other tasks on your lists, whether they're teaching or parenting related.

Here are a few ideas from other teacher-parents on how to make time for yourself:

* Schedule play dates for your kids(s) that you don't need to be present for.
* Join the YMCA or a similar organization that offers free childcare. My sister joined her local Jewish Community Center, and now she's able to go to the gym, shower, and then have some time for herself at the in-house cafe, all while her children are looked after.
* Put your kids to bed a little early when you need to.
* Wake up before your kids to get a little self-care time before the day begins.
* Schedule in something just for you. My friend takes an Irish step dancing class each week. Both she and her

husband work full time, and they have four kids under seven, but she knows it's important to nourish herself too.

× While constantly ferrying kids to different activities can be draining, it can also give you some time for yourself. When I was in high school, my mom signed all four of my younger siblings up for karate lessons at the local recreation center. It came out to only a few dollars a class, and since it was all ages, all four kids could participate at the same time. I even joined in for a year or two since I was driving them all there anyway! If you have multiple kids, prioritize activities that allow more than one of them to participate at a time.

## Higher Education

Most teachers love learning, and it's not uncommon to find full-time teachers also working on another degree or certification. I spent my first year of teaching attending graduate school two to three nights a week. In retrospect, I'm not quite sure how I did it. I woke up at 5:30 a.m. to take a bus and then a train to work, and then I took a train directly from school to downtown Chicago for three-hour classes, ending the evening close to 10:00 p.m. on a standing-room-only bus back to my apartment. I wasn't eating a single meal at home, and obviously getting far less than eight hours of sleep a night if I wanted to have anything ready for the next day. I opted not to continue the program the following year because I felt it was only hurting my teaching.

Thankfully, not all graduate programs are like this! That said, carefully consider your options before enrolling in grad school or another program. Many teachers pursue additional degrees in hopes it will help their job prospects or increase their pay. Within Chicago Public Schools, for example, having a master's degree would have increased my salary, and it would have continued to increase each year. On the other hand, if I decided to leave my current school but stay within Chicago Public Schools, it would have made me a less desirable hire because I would cost the school more money. If I had stayed at the charter school I worked at my first two years of teaching, it would not have increased my salary at all, and I would have accrued thousands of dollars of debt without any financial benefit. Of course, higher learning has rewards outside of a salary increase! Unfortunately for most teachers, however, the cost must be weighed and considered. I often come across teachers with $50,000 or more in student loan debt with no hope of paying it off any time soon. A master's degree will not automatically make you a better teacher, so if there are other ways to learn what you're hoping to learn, such as professional development or independent research, consider those options first.

But let's say you've already begun graduate school, or will begin soon, because you know it's the right path for you, financially, professionally, and personally. Like parenting, grad school will force you to spend less time on teaching, whether you like it or not, but without the reward of spending time with your own children. Here are some tips for balancing teacher life with graduate school:

- ✗ Begin at a time when you feel relatively confident in your teaching. The year you're starting at a new school or in a new grade level is not an ideal time to begin a graduate program.
- ✗ Schedule your time. There's no doubt your personal time will take a hit, but there's no reason it should disappear completely if you map out your time. Consider how much time you realistically need to spend on both teaching work and graduate work and schedule those tasks in. Be sure to schedule in self-care time as well, and stick with it! Straight A's in graduate school is not worth a mental breakdown.

* Be reasonable about the costs. I've found that, for some reason, even people who might hesitate to buy a latte in the morning have no problem accruing tens of thousands of dollars of student debt. Education is valuable, but you don't need to bankrupt yourself for it. As an undergraduate, I transferred to a state school when I learned my family would be unable to help with my tuition. My new school didn't cost me a dime after the Pell Grant (a grant for low-income students) was applied. I even got a check back each semester that helped me cover my rent. After graduation, I went on to join Teach for America, which is full of Ivy League graduates. We all ended up in the same program, but I began debt-free, while many of them had tens or even hundreds of thousands of dollars of debt. I say this not to shame anyone with debt—many of us made the decisions that would determine our student debt when we were only seventeen or eighteen years old. But you're an adult now, and the decisions you make about taking out student loans now will affect the rest of your life.

My friend Addison Duane also has some tips on what's helped her balance teaching and higher education:

*It's not lost on me, as I sit here reflecting on balancing teaching and going to graduate school, that I have lived this experience not once, but twice, in my time as a teacher. As an early career teacher, I studied part time for a Master's in Curriculum and Instruction. Now, seven years later, I am back in school full time for a nonclinical PhD in Educational Psychology. While the two grad school experiences have been drastically different, a few recurring self-care themes have emerged. What follows is a short, non-exhaustive list detailing a few tips*

I've picked up while navigating teaching, taking classes, and writing more papers than should be allowed.

**1. Take one day off every week.** *The stress of a new week often prevents me from shutting my laptop on Sundays, so Saturdays have become the day that I do nothing work- or school-related.*

**2. Schedule a short break in between the school day and the grad school work.** *For me, this means watching TV or aimlessly scrolling on my phone for a solid hour before opening my laptop to dive into reading and writing. Sometimes I'll sprinkle in doing a puzzle, calling a friend, or helping my partner cook dinner.*

**3. Sleep.** *With a to-do list that never stops growing (thanks, school), it's easy to get sucked into the idea that I need to burn the midnight oil to get everything done. This is simply not true. I am neither an effective teacher nor an engaged student when I am sleep deprived. I often joke that sleep is my favorite form of self-care because it's amazing what a good night of rest can do for my brain and body. Recently I learned that there is no such thing, scientifically, as "catching up on sleep." Getting the appropriate amount of sleep each night, instead of sleeping extra long on one weekend morning, is crucial.*

**4. Seek professional help.** *The process of finding a mental health practitioner that a) fits your budget, b) meshes well with your personality, and c) has availability when you are free can often feel like herding cats (though to be fair, I've never attempted to herd cats, so if you regularly herd cats and find it easy, let's talk). I had to sit in a few offices to find* *the right fit, and that's okay. Having an unbiased third party who can validate stressors, support problem solving, and provide ideas for maintaining my well-being, has been the most essential form of self-care for me.*

*Going to graduate school and teaching full time is an arduous task, but it's not impossible. With the right supports and the cognizance to prioritize balance and health, the experience can be both fulfilling and life-giving.*

*You can learn more from Addison on her Instagram @msduane!*

## Infertility

Before I was active in the world of teacher Instagram, I didn't realize how deeply struggling with infertility affects so many people. Many brave women have shared their struggles with getting and staying pregnant, from miscarriages to multiple rounds of IVF. As a teacher with infertility, you get up every day and love and care for other people's children, all while struggling to have your own. As a member of a profession that's mostly women, you also deal with colleagues constantly getting pregnant. One year I had seven pregnant coworkers! I did not teach while struggling with infertility myself, so I will let my friend Tamara Russell, accomplished teacher, blogger, and resource creator, take it from here:

*Infertility is trauma. It is a cycle of hurt that many women face, but that few really want to discuss. The deep sense of longing for your own child held in tension with caring for the children of others is something that I am in equal parts dismayed at and in awe of. I did it. I do it. I'm a teacher and I have battled infertility and remain childless. So, what does it look like to care for yourself during these times? For me, it was a reminder that mothering is not just the process of giving physical birth. It is the act of loving and leading children. It is the conversations where you partner with parents to keep positive momentum going at home. It is in the conversations where you're advocating for your learners to get the support in school that has been refused. It is the tenacious way that you speak up about change that is needed in the community to make it better for your students' families. It's putting Band-Aids on boo-boos and celebrating a hard-earned accomplishment with a special lunch. Self-care for me has always looked like reminding myself that I am whole as I am. I am not incomplete. Someday, the sounds of a child of my own will fill my home, and in that moment, I will remind myself that I'd been ready for this for a long time because I was already complete before this.*

*You can learn more from Tamara at mrsrussellsroom.com and on Instagram @mrsrussellsroom*

# RECOMMENDED READING

I did a lot of reading and research in preparing to write this book, and I hope it is a solid overview on how and why to practice self-care as a teacher. If you want to learn more about specific topics related to the concept of self-care, I have a few recommendations.

**On mindfulness:**
*Happy Teachers Change the World*
by Thich Nhat Hanh and Katherine Weare

**On simplifying and organizing:**
*The Life-Changing Magic of Tidying Up*
by Marie Kondo

**On anxiety:**
*The Anxiety & Phobia Workbook*
by Edmund J. Bourne

**On building habits:**
*Atomic Habits*
by James Clear

# CONCLUSION

A teacher has many roles. You are an educator, an enlightener, and an encourager, but you don't have to be a martyr. You can be a great teacher without sacrificing your well-being for your students. If you haven't discovered this already, you will learn that you can't sustain yourself on high test scores and coffee alone. You *need* to care for yourself first in order to care for others. I hope this guide has given you some ideas on how to begin or improve your self-care, but ultimately the decision is up to you to prioritize your own well-being.

# ACKNOWLEDGEMENTS

Thank you to my husband, Rob, who encouraged me throughout the process of writing this book and who never doubts that I'm capable of just about anything.

Thank you to contributors and friends Ashley Vongphakdy, Cole Yaverbaum, Becca Wertheim, Tony Romeo, LaNesha Tabb, Addison Duane, Asmahan Mashrah, and Tamara Russell for sharing their insights, especially when those insights were deeply personal.

Thank you to my first readers, Allie Szczecinski and Caitlin Bootsma.

Thank you to my therapist, Karen, who told me what I really needed to hear when I needed it most, and who has encouraged me every step of the way from stressed-out teacher to small business owner and author.

And finally, thank you to all the teachers who show up for their students, day after day, year after year. I hope this book can help you show up for yourselves too.

# REFERENCES

Amschler, Denise H., and James F. McKenzie. "Perceived Sleepiness, Sleep Habits and Sleep Concerns of Public School Teachers, Administrators and Other Personnel." *American Journal of Health Education* 41, no. 2 (January 23, 2013): 102–109. https://doi.org/10.1080/19325037.2010.10599134.

Bourne, Edmund J. *The Anxiety & Phobia Workbook*, 4th ed. Oakland, CA: New Harbinger Publications, Inc., 2005.

Carver-Thomas Desiree, and Linda Darling-Hammond. "Teacher Turnover: Why It Matters and What We Can Do About It." Learning Policy Institute, August 16, 2017. https://learningpolicyinstitute.org/product/teacher-turnover-report.

Clear, James. *Atomic Habits: An Easy & Proven Way to Build Good Habits & Break Bad Ones*. New York: Penguin Random House, 2018.

Davis, Daphne M., and Jeffrey A. Hayes. "What Are the Benefits of Mindfulness" *Monitor on Psychology* 43, no. 7 (July/August 2012). https://www.apa.org/monitor/2012/07-08/ce-corner.

Emmons, Robert A. *Thanks!: How the New Science of Gratitude Can Make You Happier*. New York: Houghton Mifflin Harcourt, 2007.

Flynn, Francis J. "Frank Flynn: Gratitude, the Gift That Keeps on Giving." Stanford Graduate School of Business, March 1, 2012. https://www.gsb.stanford.edu/insights/frank-flynn-gratitude-gift-keeps-giving.

Godoy, Maria. "From Couch Potato to Fitness Buff: How I Learned to Love Exercise." NPR.org, January 14, 2019. https://www.npr.org/sections/health-shots/2019/01/14/684118974/from-couch-potato-to-fitness-buff-how-i-learned-to-love-exercise.

Gonçalves, J. P. B., G. Lucchetti, P. R. Menezes, and H. Vallada. "Religious and Spiritual Interventions in Mental Health Care: A Systematic Review and

Meta-Analysis of Randomized Controlled Clinical Trials." *Psychological Medicine* 45, no. 14 (October 2015): 2937–49. https://doi.org/10.1017/S0033291715001166.

Hanh, Thich Nhat, and Katherine Weare. *Happy Teachers Change the World: A Guide for Cultivating Mindfulness in Education*. Berkeley, California: Parallax Press, 2017.

Herman, Keith C., Jal'et Hickmon-Rosa, and Wendy M. Reinke. "Empirically Derived Profiles of Teacher Stress, Burnout, Self-Efficacy, and Coping and Associated Student Outcomes." *Journal of Positive Behavior Interventions* 20, no. 2 (April 1 2018): 90–100. https://doi.org/10.1177/1098300717732066

Johns Hopkins Medicine. "Is There Really Any Benefit to Multivitamins?" The Johns Hopkins University, The Johns Hopkins Hospital, and Johns Hopkins Health System. Accessed November 7, 2019. www.hopkinsmedicine.org/health/wellness-and-prevention/is-there-really-any-benefit-to-multivitamins.

Ingersoll, Richard M., Elizabeth Merrill, Daniel Stuckey, and Gregory Collins. "Seven Trends: The Transformation of the Teaching Force." *CPRE Research Reports*, November 13, 2018. https://repository.upenn.edu/cpre_researchreports/108.

Klein, Kitty, and Adriel Boals. "Expressive Writing Can Increase Working Memory Capacity." *Journal of Experimental Psychology: General* 130, no. 3 (2001): 520–33. https://doi.org/10.1037/0096-3445.130.3.520.

Klussman, U., M. Kunter, U. Trautwein, O. Ludtke, and J. Baumert. "Teachers' Occupational Well-Being and Quality of Instruction: The Important Role of Self-Regulatory Patterns." *Journal of Educational Psychology* 100, no. 3 (2008): 702–15.

Krpan, Katherine M., Ethan Kross, Marc G. Berman, Patricia J. Deldin, Mary K. Askren, and John Jonides. "An Everyday Activity as a Treatment for Depression: The Benefits of Expressive Writing for People Diagnosed with Major Depressive Disorder." *Journal of Affective Disorders* 150, no. 3 (September 25, 2013). https://doi.org/10.1016/j.jad.2013.05.065.

Kubey, Robert, and Mihaly Csikszentmihalyi. "Television Addiction Is No Mere Metaphor." *Scientific American* 286, no. 2 (March 2002): 74–80.

Leiter, M. P., and P. Harvie. "The Correspondence of Supervisor and Subordinate Perspectives on Major Organizational Change." *Journal of Occupational Health Psychology* 2 (October 1997): 343–52.

Maslach, Christina, and Michael P. Leiter. "Early Predictors of Job Burnout and Engagement." *Journal of Applied Psychology* 93, no. 3 (May 2008): 498–512.

Maslach, Christina, and Michael P. Leiter. *The Truth About Burnout: How Organizations Cause Personal Stress and What to Do about It*. San Francisco: Jossey-Bass, 1997.

Murray, Bridget. "Writing to Heal." *Monitor on Psychology* 33, no. 6 (June 2002). https://www.apa.org/monitor/jun02/writing.

Nathanson, Rick. "Lawsuit Filed over Sick Leave Policy for NM Teachers." *Las Cruces Sun-News*, April 17, 2017. https://www.lcsun-news.com/story/news/education/2017/04/17/lawsuit-filed-over-sick-leave-policy-nm-teachers/100565664/.

The National Academies of Sciences, Engineering, and Medicine. "Report Sets Dietary Intake Levels for Water, Salt, and Potassium to Maintain Health and Reduce Chronic Disease Risk." News release, February 11, 2004. https://www.nationalacademies.org/news/2004/02/report-sets-dietary-intake-levels-for-water-salt-and-potassium-to-maintain-health-and-reduce-chronic-disease-risk.

Seabrook, Elizabeth M., Margaret L. Kern, and Nikki S. Rickard. "Social Networking Sites, Depression, and Anxiety: A Systematic Review." *JMIR Mental Health* 3, no. 4 (2016): e50. https://doi.org/10.2196/mental.5842.

Selye, Hans. *Stress without Distress*. United Kingdom: McClelland and Stewart, 1974.

Skovholt, Thomas M., and Michelle Trotter-Mathison. *The Resilient Practitioner: Burnout and Compassion Fatigue Prevention and Self-Care Strategies for the Helping Professions*, 3rd ed. New York: Routledge, 2016.

Substance Abuse and Mental Health Services Administration. *Key Substance Use and Mental Health Indicators in the United States: Results from the 2018 National Survey on Drug Use and Health* (HHS Publication No. PEP19-5068, NSDUH Series H-54). Rockville, MD: Center for Behavioral Health Statistics and Quality, Substance Abuse and Mental Health Services Administration, 2019. Retrieved from https://www.samhsa.gov/data/.

Wexler, Natalie. "Why Homework Doesn't Seem to Boost Learning—And How It Could." *Forbes*, January 3, 2019. https://www.forbes.com/sites/nataliewexler/2019/01/03/why-homework-doesnt-seem-to-boost-learning-and-how-it-could/.

World Health Organization. "Burn-out an 'Occupational Phenomenon': International Classification of Diseases." Accessed November 11, 2019. http://www.who.int/mental_health/evidence/burn-out/en/.

# ABOUT THE AUTHOR

Sarah Forst is passionate about helping teachers be the best educators they can be *without* sacrificing their well-being. As a former special education teacher in Chicago Public Schools, she learned the importance of teacher self-care the hard way. She strives to help teachers every day through her self-care subscription box for teachers, Teacher Care Crate, and meaningful classroom resources in her online store, The Designer Teacher.

Visit Sarah at:
**THEDESIGNERTEACHER.COM**
Instagram: @thedesignerteacher
Facebook: The Designer Teacher

If you enjoyed *The Teacher's Guide to Self-Care*, please help other teachers discover this book by leaving a review at Amazon.com and Goodreads.com.

Made in the USA
Columbia, SC
13 August 2021